Money Laundering and Terrorist Financing
Act 2010: Annotated

GW00597252

Money Laundering and Terrorist Financing Act 2010: Annotated

Criminal Justice (Money Laundering and Terrorist Financing) Act 2010

By
Dr Max Barrett
LL.B., Ph.D., Dip. Arb.,
Dip. Int. Arb., Dip. FSL, Solicitor

CLARUS PRESS

Published by
Clarus Press Ltd,
Griffith Campus,
South Circular Road,
Dublin 8.

Typeset by
Datapage International Limited,
157 Rathmines Road Upper,
Rathmines,
Dublin 6.

Printed by
CPI Anthony Rowe,
Chippenham,
Willtshire,
UK.

ISBN
978-1-905536-35-1

All materials reproduced with the kind permission of the Oireachtas.

Disclaimer
Whilst every effort has been made to ensure that the contents of this book are
accurate, neither the publisher nor author can accept responsibility for any
errors or omissions or loss occasioned to any person acting or refraining
from acting as result of any material in this publication.

Για την Αγάπη

PREFACE

"'And nobody's getting rich?'
'That's a good point you've put your finger on, Thomas. Somebody *ought* to be getting rich. Somebody ought to be *seen* to be getting rich. But that part of it's very cleverly arranged. Big wins on race courses, investments in stocks and shares, all things which are natural, just chancy enough to make big money at, and all apparently genuine transactions. There's a lot of money stacked up abroad in different countries and different places. It's a great big, vast, money-making concern – and the money's always on the move – going from place to place.'
'Well,' said Tommy, 'good luck to you. I hope you get your man.'"

Agatha Christie, *By The Pricking Of My Thumbs*, Ch.12.

The goal of many criminal acts is to generate a profit for the person or persons engaged in those acts. Money laundering involves the processing of criminal profits so as to disguise their illegal origin. Money laundering is a predicate criminal offence, *i.e.* it cannot occur unless there has first been a criminal act that has given rise to criminal proceeds which can be laundered. Typically there are three stages to money laundering:

– *placement*

In the placement stage the launderer introduces his criminal proceeds into the financial system. There are a wide variety of steps that could be taken at this stage. For example, a launderer might break up large sums of money into smaller, less conspicuous amounts that are deposited into myriad accounts. Or he could purchase money instruments in one location that are deposited into accounts in another location. This stage often takes place in the country where the funds originate.

– *layering*

In the layering stage the launderer engages in a series of transactions that seek to distance the funds from their source. So, for example, the launderer may transfer the funds through a series of accounts across multiple jurisdictions. He may also, for example, seek to disguise the transfers as payments for goods or services in a bid to legitimise them. This stage could involve anywhere with a suitable financial services infrastructure.

– *integration*

This is where the monies re-enter the legitimate economy as the launderer uses his layered funds to purchase a lifestyle with his formerly "dirty" money. This stage may also take place away from the jurisdiction where the criminal profits were earned.

Money laundering can occur anywhere in the world but, for obvious reasons, money launderers are typically attracted to jurisdictions and sectors where there is a low risk of discovery. However, because they want their "dirty" money (or most of it) back once laundered, launderers also have a preference to move funds through stable financial centres.

The Financial Action Task Force on money laundering (FATF), established by the G7 countries in 1989, suggests that money laundering is bad for legitimate business, bad for economic progress and bad for society generally (see generally the FATF website at *www.fatf-gafi.org*).

Legitimate business

Money laundering may be good for launderers. However, the FATF suggests that it is bad for legitimate businesses, particularly those in the financial services sector. If funds from criminal activity can be easily processed through a particular financial centre or institution it is only a short step to complicity and active criminality. Such complicity/criminality is bad in itself but, if unchecked, can quickly tarnish the reputation and profitability of the relevant financial centre or institution.

Economic progress

Money laundering, per the FATF, also has the potential to be bad for economies in that foreign direct investment will be negatively impacted where a country's financial service providers are perceived to be complicit in criminality. So combating money laundering is not just right in itself but something for which there is a clear economic imperative.

Society generally

Money laundering, per the FATF, can also be bad for society if criminals are allowed to infiltrate the financial sector, invest widely in the economy and perhaps engage in bribery and corruption. At a more basic level, unchecked money laundering allows criminals to enjoy the fruits of their criminal behaviour, making it attractive for them and others to commit more crimes.

However, money laundering is not all good for criminals. It is often by following financial records established in the course of money laundering that law enforcement agencies are able to discover the architects and perpetrators of crime. They are also of course able to locate the proceeds of crime and ensure that criminals can be deprived of them.

Through the establishment of a comprehensive anti-money laundering regime States can increase the awareness of money laundering and provide the necessary legal and regulatory tools to combat what is a serious crime. The Criminal Justice (Money Laundering and Terrorist Financing) Act 2010 (hereafter the "Act") seeks to put Ireland's existing anti-money laundering and anti-terrorist financing regime on a new footing so that the Irish legal system accords with the requirements of the Third Money Laundering Directive and is better placed to deal with the ever-changing forms of money laundering and terrorist financing.

As its title suggests, the Act is concerned both with money laundering and also with terrorist financing. Terrorist offences are similar to money laundering offences in that they do not respect frontiers. A terrorist group may, for example, target a Government in one country, yet maintain its funds in the financial institutions of another country. It follows that an international response is required to what is an international problem.

In Ireland, the Criminal Justice (Terrorist Offences) Act 2005 has given effect under Irish law to a number of international instruments directed at terrorism and has enabled (and enables) Ireland to meet the anti-terrorism commitments which Ireland has undertaken, both as a member state of the European Union and as a member of the wider international community, including commitments arising from United Nations Security Resolution 1373 (adopted in response to the 9/11 attack on the United States).

The detail of what constitutes terrorist financing for the purposes of the 2005 Act is considered elsewhere in this text but broadly it comprises what the colloquial term would suggest, *i.e.* providing, collecting or receiving funds that will be used to carry out terrorist acts or for the benefit or purposes of a terrorist group.

The 2005 Act "sandwiched" an anti-terrorist dimension into the previously existing anti-money laundering regime extant under the Criminal Justice Act 1994, as amended, requiring, for example, that a designated body (now supplanted in the Act by a designated person) adopt measures to prevent and detect the commission of an offence of financing terrorism, train staff to identify transactions which might relate to such an offence, and report suspicions that an offence of financing terrorism had been or was being committed.

As with other organised criminal groups, a terrorist group's income may be derived from crimes such as kidnapping, extortion, smuggling, fraud, theft, drug trafficking, *etc*. The laundering of the proceeds of those crimes could reasonably be expected to be caught by the anti-money laundering regime. However, there are aspects of terrorist financing that would not constitute money laundering. For example, fundraising activities may be carried out in the name of charitable or relief organisations that are a front for a terrorist group. This fundraising could be done by way of collection of subscriptions, sale of publications, speaking tours, cultural or social events, door-to-door solicitation, appeals for funds to wealthy donors and donations by persons of a portion of their earnings to a particular group. In short, whereas money laundering is concerned with "dirty money", terrorist financing can involve "clean money" and also relatively small sums of money.

The Act updates the existing monitoring, reporting and training regime applicable to terrorist financing but otherwise leaves the 2005 Act broadly intact, a decision that attracted some comment during the Oireachtas debates that preceded the enactment of the Act, with one Senator suggesting that a more comprehensive consolidation of the law applicable to money laundering, terrorist financing (and perhaps also the financial sanctions regime, though this was not mentioned) would have been preferable. An annotated version of such a consolidated Act may fall to be written at some future time. For now, practitioners must contend with the Act.

This annotated version of the Act is written as of 15 October 2010. The usual disclaimer applies.

Max Barrett

15 October 2010

Criminal Justice (Money Laundering and Terrorist Financing) Act 2010

(No. 6 of 2010)

ARRANGEMENT OF SECTIONS

PART 1

Preliminary

PART 2

Money Laundering Offences

PART 3

Directions, Orders and Authorisations Relating to Investigations

PART 4

Provisions Relating to Finance Services Industry, Professional Service Providers and Others

Chapter 1

Interpretation (Part 4)

Chapter 2

Designation of places other than Member States — procedures for detecting money laundering or terrorist financing

Chapter 3

Customer Due Diligence

Chapter 4

Reporting of suspicious transactions and of transactions involving certain places

Chapter 5

Tipping off by designated persons

Chapter 6

Internal policies and procedures, training and record keeping

Chapter 7

Special provisions applying to credit and financial institutions

Chapter 8

Monitoring of designated persons

Chapter 9

Authorisation of Trust or Company Service Providers

Chapter 10

Other

PART 5

Miscellaneous

SCHEDULE 1

Revocations of Statutory Instruments

SCHEDULE 2

Annex I to Recast Banking Consolidation Directive
List of Activities subject to Mutual Recognition

AN ACT TO PROVIDE FOR OFFENCES OF, AND RELATED TO, MONEY LAUNDERING IN AND OUTSIDE THE STATE; TO GIVE EFFECT TO DIRECTIVE 2005/60/EC OF THE EUROPEAN PARLIAMENT AND OF THE COUNCIL OF 26 OCTOBER 2005 ON THE PREVENTION OF THE USE OF THE FINANCIAL SYSTEM FOR THE PURPOSE OF MONEY LAUNDERING AND TERRORIST FINANCING; TO PROVIDE FOR THE REGISTRATION OF PERSONS DIRECTING PRIVATE MEMBERS' CLUBS; TO PROVIDE FOR THE AMENDMENT OF THE CENTRAL BANK ACT 1942 AND THE COURTS (SUPPLEMENTAL PROVISIONS) ACT 1961; TO PROVIDE FOR THE CONSEQUENTIAL REPEAL OF CERTAIN PROVISIONS OF THE CRIMINAL JUSTICE ACT 1994; THE CONSEQUENTIAL AMEND-MENT OF CERTAIN ENACTMENTS AND THE REVOCATION OF CERTAIN STATUTORY INSTRUMENTS; AND TO PROVIDE FOR RELATED MATTERS.

[5TH MAY, 2010]

General Note

The Act was signed into law by President Mary McAleese on 5 May 2010. It has as its principal purpose the implementation of the Third Money Laundering Directive, *i.e.* Directive 2005/60/EC of the European Parliament and of the Council of 26 October 2005 (hereafter the "Directive") on the prevention of the use of the financial system for the purpose of money laundering and terrorist financing. (O.J. L309, 25.11.2005, p. 15), as amended. Art.45(1) of the Directive requires that the Directive be implemented in each Member State by 15 December 2007. However, it was not until almost two years after this date – on 19 November 2009 – that the Minister for Justice, Equality and Law Reform (Deputy Dermot Ahern) introduced the Criminal Justice (Money Laundering and Terrorist Financing) Bill 2009 (No. 55 of 2009, hereafter the "Bill") before Dáil Éireann. In the meantime, the European Commission had obtained two judgments against Ireland in the European Court of Justice, one on 19 May 2009 (Case C-532/08) and another on 1 October 2009 (Case C-549/08). Both cases were brought under Art.226 of the EC Treaty for failure to fulfil obligations. The first case was concerned with Ireland's failure to implement the Directive. The second was concerned with Ireland's failure to implement the Commission Directive referred to in the Act as the "Implementing Directive". In both cases the Court of Justice held that there was a failure by Ireland to fulfil its obligation to implement the directives and awarded costs against Ireland. The judgment in each case is interesting because of the behind-the-scenes detail as to what the Irish Government was contending in its dealings with the European Commission. Per the Court in Case C-549/08 (at p.1):

"(2) Pursuant to Article 5 of [the Implementing Directive] ... Member States were required to bring into force the laws, regulations and administrative provisions necessary to comply with the Directive by 15 December 2007 at the latest and to inform the Commission thereof.

(3) Having received no notification concerning the measures adopted by Ireland to transpose [the Implementing Directive] ... into its national law, and in the absence of any other information from which it could conclude that Ireland had fulfilled its obligation to do so, the Commission initiated the infringement procedure provided by Article 226 EC, and by letter of 28 January 2008, formally called on Ireland to submit its observations within two months of receipt of that letter.

(4) By letter of 19 March 2008, the Irish authorities replied that they were not yet in a position to notify the transposing measures, but that the drafting of a bill had been approved and that a public consultation process had been set in motion. It was hoped to have the transposing legislation published and introduced in Parliament during the summer session.

(5) Having received no information confirming that [the Implementing Directive] ... had been transposed, the Commission, by letter of 6 June 2008, sent Ireland a reasoned opinion calling on it to take the measures necessary to comply with the obligations under that directive within two months of receipt of that opinion.

(6) By letter of 29 July 2008, Ireland stated that the public consultation process had been concluded, that the legislative process was underway and that the transposing measures in question had been included in the legislative programme for the autumn parliamentary session.

(7) Having received no further notification from the Irish authorities concerning the adoption of those transposing measures, the Commission brought the present action.

(8) In its defence, Ireland does not contest the allegation that it has failed to fulfil its obligations, but submits that the transposing legislation will be enacted by 31 July 2009. It asks the Court to suspend the proceedings for a period of eight months."

The European Commission successfully opposed the application for suspension and the Court held that Ireland was in breach of its obligations. Seven weeks after this judgment was delivered, the Bill was introduced before the Oireachtas.

The long title to the Act does not expand greatly on the rationale for the Act. The Minister for Justice, Equality and Law Reform, at the Second Reading Stage of the Bill expanded on its purpose, stating:

> "The main purpose of the Bill before the House today is to transpose the third EU money laundering and terrorist financing directive into Irish law and to comply with the recommendations of the financial action task force, FATF, third round mutual evaluation report on Ireland. The Bill will also give effect to certain provisions of the United Nations Convention Against Transnational Organized Crime." (695(2) *Díospóireachtaí Parlaiminte* (19.11.2009), p.259).

A brief overview of the Directive, the FATF, the third round mutual evaluation report and the UN Convention Against Transnational Organized Crime follows.

The Directive
At the European level, the first anti-money laundering directive (Council Directive 91/308/EEC of 10 June 1991 on prevention of the use of the financial system for the purpose of money laundering (O.J. L166, 28.6.1991, p.77)) was adopted in 1991, the second (Directive 2001/97/EC of the European Parliament and of the Council of 4 December 2001 amending Council Directive 91/308/EEC on prevention of the use of the financial system for the purpose of money laundering (O.J. L344, 28.12.2009, p.76)) in 2001 and the third (the Directive) in 2005. The recitals to the Directive identify a variety of reasons as to why its adoption was necessary and thus are of interest in better understanding the rationale for the Act. Various of the rationales offered in the Directive for anti-money laundering and anti-terrorist financing legislation per se (as opposed to rationales offered for EU-level legislation in this area) are outlined below:

    – recital (1) refers to the fact that massive flows of "dirty money" can damage the stability and reputation of the financial sector and threaten the single market, while terrorism shakes the very foundations of society; criminalising such behaviour and also taking a preventive effort via the financial system is considered an effective means of combating these difficulties;

    – recital (5) indicates that anti-money laundering and anti-terrorist financing legislation ought to be consistent with advancing international standards such as the revised FATF Recommendations (considered hereafter), offering a further reason for revised legislation;

    – recital (9) refers to the fact that the previous Directive in this area, while it imposed a customer identification obligation, contained relatively little detail on procedures, stating that "it is appropriate, in accordance with the new international standards, to introduce more specific and detailed provisions relating to the identification of the customer and of any beneficial owner and the verification of their identity", adding that a detailed definition of who constitutes a "beneficial owner" is therefore required;

- recital (15) mentions the need to extend anti-money laundering and anti-terrorist financing legislation to life insurance intermediaries and trust and company service providers given the practical experience that tightening of controls in the financial sector is apparently prompting money launderers and terrorist financiers to seek alternative methods of going about their business;

- recital (22) points to the need to recognise that the risk of money-laundering and terrorist financing is not the same in every case and that in line with a risk-based approach the principle of simplified customer due diligence in appropriate cases ought to be introduced into law;

- recital (24) points to the need for legislation to recognise that certain situations present a heightened risk of money laundering or terrorist financing and require particularly rigorous customer identification and verification procedures. (Recital (25) refers specifically to politically exposed persons in this regard);

- recital (27) points to the need to avoid repeated customer identification "leading to delays and inefficiency in business" and highlights the appropriateness of allowing customers whose identification has been ascertained (and presumably verified) elsewhere to be introduced by a third party, though without prejudice to the respective liabilities of identifier and "designated person" to identify their own customers;

- recital (32) refers to the need for Member States to protect employees who report suspicions of money laundering (the recital does not mention terrorist financing) from threats and hostile action;

- recital (35) points to the need for what is in effect an extra-jurisdictional application of the Directive given that "[m]oney laundering and terrorist financing are international problems and the effort to combat them should be global";

- recital (37) points to the fact that the Directive establishes detailed rules both for customer due diligence and also for compliance management procedures and policies;

- recital (39) points to (and the Directive contains) a requirement that when, for example, registering a trust and company service provider (a "trust or company service provider" in the Act) competent authorities should ensure that the persons who effectively direct or will direct the business of such entities and the beneficial owners of such entities are "fit and proper persons".

The reference in the twenty-second recital to a risk-based approach to customer and due diligence ("CDD") is one of the principal distinguishing features between the Directive and the EU measures that preceded it. In effect the Directive (and, pursuant thereto, the Act) allow designated persons to determine, for example, the appropriate CDD measures to apply by reference to particular risks arising. However, it is possible that designated persons may consider their freedom of action constrained in this regard by reference to any guidelines approved under s.107 of the Act and/or the extent to which the competent authority responsible for monitoring the relevant designated person considers rigorous compliance with any (if any) approved guidelines applicable to that designated person to be desirable. There is also the additional difficulty that a risk-based approach to terrorist financing is singularly difficult to achieve given that the funds in question may be "clean money" (*i.e.* not the proceeds of criminal conduct), the amounts involved may be very small, and the activities involved (*e.g.* fundraising or the purchase of particular products such as chemicals) can appear entirely innocent.

FATF

Sophisticated money laundering schemes often have a cross-border dimension. Because of this, international cooperation is essential to combating it, and has been forthcoming. International organisations such as the United Nations and the Bank for International Settlements took steps in this regard at the end of the 1980s. However, matters took a significant leap forwards with the establishment by the G7 countries of the Financial Action Task Force (FATF) in 1989. In 1990, the original FATF 40 Recommendations were drawn up by the FATF as part of an effort to combat the laundering of drug money. The 40 Recommendations, as their title suggests, seek to identify best practices for countries to adopt in the context of combating money laundering. In 1996 the initial Recommendations were revised to reflect changing money laundering typologies. In the years since then the FATF Recommendations have been adopted by almost 150 countries. In October 2001 (a month after the 9/11 attacks in the United States), the FATF expanded its role to deal with the issue of terrorist financing. Following the approach adopted with regard to drug money in the preceding decade it adopted first Eight and now Nine Special Recommendations on Terrorist Financing which are complementary to the 40 Recommendations but focused instead on terrorist financing. The FATF 40 Recommendations and the Nine Special Recommendations have been recognised by the International Monetary Fund and the World Bank as the international standards for combating money laundering and terrorist financing.

As well as seeking to adhere to the various FATF Recommendations, FATF members (of which there are, at the time of writing, 36) subscribe to a system of mutual evaluation. This is considered by the FATF to be a vital component in ensuring that its various recommendations are effectively implemented by member countries. The report that followed the last FATF review of Ireland was published in February 2006. (See FATF, *Third Mutual Evaluation/Detailed Assessment Report (Ireland)* (17 February 2006), hereafter the "Report"). It found that Ireland had a broadly satisfactory legal framework in place to combat money laundering and terrorist financing. However, it pointed *inter alia* to the low number of convictions obtained in this context. Per the Report (at p.6):

> "Between 2001 and 2004 inclusive, 15 people were charged with ML [money laundering] and 8 people have been convicted. Sentences being handed down on conviction generally appear appropriate (from 2 to 5 years imprisonment). There have been a relatively low number of convictions. A lack of comprehensive statistics on ML investigations, prosecutions and convictions prevents a full evaluation of effectiveness. There have been no prosecutions for TF [terrorist financing]...".

United Nations Convention Against Transnational Organized Crime (the Palermo Convention)
The thirty-fifth of the FATF 40 Recommendations recommends that:

> "Countries should take immediate steps to become party to and implement fully the Vienna Convention, the Palermo Convention, and the 1999 United Nations International Convention for the Suppression of the Financing of Terrorism. Countries are also encouraged to ratify and implement other relevant international conventions, such as the 1990 Council of Europe Convention on Laundering, Search, Seizure and Confiscation of the Proceeds from Crime...". (FATF, *FATF 40 Recommendations*, p.12).

The Conventions, other than the Palermo Convention, referred to above are: (1) the United Nations Convention against Illicit Traffic in Narcotic Drugs and Psychotropic Substances done at Vienna on 20 October 1998 (the Vienna Convention). (This was signed on behalf of Ireland on 14 December 1989, ratified by Ireland on 3 September 1996 and entered into force with respect to Ireland on 2 December 1996 (see Treaty Series 1997, No. 4)); (2) the International Convention for the Suppression of the Financing of Terrorism done at New York on 9 December 2009. (This was signed on behalf of Ireland on 15 January 2001, the instrument of ratification was deposited with the Secretary-General of the United Nations on 1 July 2005 and entered into force with respect to Ireland on 30 July 2005 (see Treaty Series 2006, No. 10)); and (3) the Council of Europe Convention on Laundering, Search, Seizure and Confiscation of the Proceeds from Crime done at Warsaw on 16 May 2005. (The European Community signed this Convention on 2 April 2009).

The United Nations Convention Against Transnational Organized Crime was signed in Palermo in December 2000. The Convention was signed on behalf of Ireland on 13 December 2000 and ratified by Ireland on 17 June 2010. The central notion which underpins the Convention is that if criminals have embraced the globalised economy and the sophisticated technology that goes with it, then states must of necessity adopt a less fragmented and more global response to the threat posed by such international crime. The Convention requires that states which are party thereto inter alia:

(1) criminalise participation in an organised criminal group (Art.5);
(2) criminalise the laundering of proceeds of crime (Art.6);
(3) adopt measures to combat money laundering (Art.7);
(4) criminalise and take other measures against corruption (Arts.8 and 9);
(5) make participation in serious crimes involving an organised group criminal, civil or administrative wrongs (Art.10);
(6) take steps to ensure due prosecution and adjudication of, and sanctions for, various of the foregoing wrongs, including money laundering (Art.11);
(7) adopt measures to facilitate confiscation and seizure (Art.12);
(8) facilitate confiscation by other states and make other provision as regards confiscation (Arts.13 and 14);
(9) establish jurisdiction in domestic and extra-jurisdictional instances of various of the offences established in accordance with the Convention (Art.15);
(10) facilitate extradition for various offences (Art.16);
(11) offer wide mutual assistance in investigations, prosecutions and judicial proceedings relating to various crimes (Art.18);
(12) consider concluding international agreements for the establishment of joint investigative bodies in offences with an international dimension (Art.19);
(13) insofar as a signatory's legal system permits, adopt special investigative techniques so as to effectively combat organised crime (Art.20);
(14) consider the possibility of transferring criminal proceedings between them where such transfer is in the interests of the proper administration of justice (Art.21);
(15) adopt measures criminalising the obstruction of justice (Art.23);
(16) provide for adequate protection of witnesses giving testimony concerning offences covered by the Convention (Art.24);
(17) take appropriate measures to encourage cooperation with law enforcement authorities by persons who participate/d in organised criminal groups (Art.26);
(18) cooperate with each other to enhance the effectiveness of law enforcement action to combat the offences covered by the Convention (Art.27);
(19) take specified steps as regards the collection, exchange and analysis of information on the nature of organised crime (Art.28);
(20) provide suitable training and technical assistance for their respective law enforcers (Art.29);
(21) take measures conducive to the optimal implementation of the Convention (Art.30);
(22) endeavour to take certain steps aimed at the prevention of transnational organised crime (Art.31);

(23) report as indicated to a Conference of the Parties to the Convention established to improve the capacity of such states, *inter alia*, to combat transnational organised crime;

(24) take the necessary measures to ensure implementation of their respective obligations under the Convention (Art.34); and

(25) endeavour to settle certain Convention-related disputes through negotiation (Art.35).

In addition states that are party to the Convention may: consider entering into agreements or arrangements for the international transfer of sentenced persons (Art.17); and adopt measures for taking previous offences of an accused in another state into account in criminal proceedings for an offence covered by the Convention (Art.22).

Items (2), (3), (6) and (9) are directly addressed in the Act. The Act can be viewed as a step/measure of a type referred to in any of (21), (22) and (24).

Private members' clubs
There has been a proliferation in Ireland in recent years of private members' clubs providing casino-style games to club members on the basis that the provisions of the Gaming and Lotteries Act 1956 (No. 2 of 1956), as amended, do not apply to bona fide members' clubs. (See further the Report of the Casino Committee, "Regulating Gaming in Ireland" (2008)). In addition to implementing the Directive, the Act provides for the registration of any person, acting in Ireland in the course of business carried on by that person in Ireland, who effectively directs a private members' club at which gambling activities are carried on.

Partial consolidation
The Act goes some way towards consolidating existing anti-money laundering and terrorist financing legislation. However, it stops short of full consolidation, leaving extant sections of the Criminal Justice Act 1994 (previously the mainstay of the Irish anti-money laundering and anti-terrorist financing regime) and the Criminal Justice (Terrorist Offences) Act 2005. Speaking in this regard during the Second Stage reading by the Seanad of the Bill Senator Ivana Bacik stated:

> "The Minister...referred to the consolidating nature of this Bill. It certainly refers to a great deal of earlier legislation and repeals a large number of regulations....It is somewhat regrettable, however, that the opportunity was not taken in the Bill to do a proper consolidating or codifying job....Unfortunately, in this area of money laundering offences and terrorist financing we still have a range of legislation dealing with it. The Bill amends various provisions of the Criminal Justice Act but it does not repeal the Act in total and, in a way, that is regrettable." (201(4) *Díospóir-eachtaí Parlaiminte* (Seanad Éireann) (2.3.10), p.219).

Citation

Criminal Justice (Money Laundering and Terrorist Financing) Act 2010. (Per s.1(1) of the Act).

Commencement Date

15 July 2010. (Per Criminal Justice (Money Laundering and Terrorist Financing) Act 2010 (Commencement) Order 2010. (S.I. No. 342 of 2010)).

Secondary legislation

At the time of writing, the secondary legislation listed below has been adopted under the Act:

- Criminal Justice (Money Laundering and Terrorist Financing) Act 2010 (Commencement) Order 2010.
  (S.I. No. 342 of 2010). Appoints 15 July 2010 as the day on which the Act came into operation.
- Criminal Justice (Money Laundering and Terrorist Financing) Act 2010 (Section 31) Order 2010.
  (S.I. No. 343 of 2010). Designates the following places for the purposes of s.31: Argentina; Australia; Brazil; Canada; Hong Kong; Iceland; Japan; Liechtenstein; Mexico; New Zealand; Norway; Russian Federation; Singapore; Switzerland; South Africa; the United States of America; the Channel Islands; the Isle of Man; the Dutch overseas territories of Netherlands Antilles and Aruba; and the French overseas territories of Mayotte, New Caledonia, French Polynesia, Saint Pierre and Miquelon and Wallis and Futuna.
- European Communities (Trust or Company Service Providers) (Temporary Authorisation) Regulations 2010.
  (S.I. No. 347 of 2010). Introduce certain transitional measures that streamline the initial authorisation application process under s.88 of the Act.
- Trust or Company Service Provider (Authorisation) (Fees) Regulations 2010.
  (S.I. No. 348 of 2010). Prescribe €130 as the fee that must accompany an application made under s.88 of the Act or s.92 of the Act.

Parliamentary History

Dáil Éireann

Order for Second Stage, 695(2) *Díospóireachtaí Parlaiminte*, 19.12.2009, p. 259.

Second Stage, 695(2) *Díospóireachtaí Parlaiminte*, 19.12.2009, pp. 259-284.

Referral to Select Committee, 695(2) *Díospóireachtaí Parlaiminte*, 19.12.2009, p. 284.

Select Committee on Justice, Equality, Defence and Women's Rights, 14.1.2010.

Order for Report Stage, 702(3) *Díospóireachtaí Parlaiminte*, 17.2.2010, p. 567.
Report and Final Stages, 702(3) *Díospóireachtaí Parlaiminte*, 17.2.2010, pp. 567-575.
Committee of the House, 707(4) *Díospóireachtaí Parlaiminte*, 28.4.2010, pp. 637-651.

Seanad Éireann
Second Stage, 201(4) *Díospóireachtaí Parlaiminte*, 2.3.2010, pp. 203-227.
Committee Stage, 201(9) *Díospóireachtaí Parlaiminte*, 11.3.2010, pp.586-598.
Report and Final Stages, 202(2) *Díospóireachtaí Parlaiminte*, 21.4.2010, pp. 70-82.

Acts Referred to

Bail Act 1997	1997, No. 16
Central Bank Act 1942	1942, No. 22
Central Bank Act 1997	1997, No. 8
Central Bank and Financial Services Authority of Ireland Act 2003	2003, No. 12
Central Bank and Financial Services Authority of Ireland Act 2004	2004, No. 21
Civil Service Regulation Act 1956	1956, No. 46
Companies Acts	
Companies (Auditing and Accounting) Act 2003	2003, No. 44
Courts (Supplemental Provisions) Act 1961	1961, No. 39
Credit Union Act 1997	1997, No. 15
Criminal Justice Act 1994	1994, No. 15
Criminal Justice Act 2006	2006, No. 26
Criminal Justice (Mutual Assistance) Act 2008	2008, No. 7
Criminal Justice (Miscellaneous Provisions) Act 2009	2009, No. 28
Criminal Justice (Surveillance) Act 2009	2009, No. 19
Criminal Justice (Terrorist Offences) Act 2005	2005, No. 2
Criminal Justice (Theft and Fraud Offences) Act 2001	2001, No. 50
Criminal Law Act 1997	1997, No. 14
Data Protection Acts 1988 and 2003	
European Arrest Warrant Act 2003	2003, No. 45
Extradition Act 1965	1965, No. 17
Finance Act 2004	2004, No. 8
Finance Act 2006	2006, No. 6
Freedom of Information Act 1997	1997, No. 13
Investment Intermediaries Act 1995	1995, No. 11
Investor Compensation Act 1998	1998, No. 37

Mercantile Marine Act 1955	1955, No. 29
Partnership Act 1890	53 & 54 Vic., c. 39
Solicitors (Amendment) Act 1994	1994, No. 27
Taxes Consolidation Act 1997	1997, No. 39
Taxi Regulation Act 2003	2003, No. 25

Be it enacted by the Oireachtas as follows:

PART 1

Preliminary

Short title and commencement

1.—(1) This Act may be cited as the Criminal Justice (Money Laundering and Terrorist Financing) Act 2010.

(2) This Act shall come into operation on such day or days as may be appointed by order or orders made by the Minister, either generally or with reference to a particular purpose or provision, and different days may be so appointed for different purposes and different provisions.

(3) An order under *subsection (2)* may, in respect of the repeal of the provisions of the Criminal Justice Act 1994 specified in *section 4*, and the revocation of the statutory instruments specified in *Schedule 1* effected by *section 4(2)*, appoint different days for the repeal of different provisions of the Criminal Justice Act 1994 and the revocation of different statutory instruments or different provisions of them.

Section Note

Section 1 states the short title of the Act and identifies the process whereby the Act may be brought into operation. In the Criminal Justice (Money Laundering and Terrorist Financing) Act 2010 (Commencement) Order 2010 (S.I. No. 342 of 2010) the Minister for Justice and Law Reform appointed 15 July 2010 as the day on which the entirety of the Act came into operation.

Interpretation

2.—(1) In this Act—

"Implementing Directive" means Commission Directive 2006/70/EC of 1 August 2006 laying down implementing measures for Directive 2005/60/EC of the European Parliament and of the Council as regards the definition of "politically exposed person" and the technical criteria for simplified customer due diligence procedures and for exemption on grounds of a financial activity conducted on an occasional or very limited basis;[1]

"Minister" means the Minister for Justice, Equality and Law Reform;

"money laundering" means an offence under *Part 2*;

"prescribed" means prescribed by the Minister by regulations made under this Act;

"property" means all real or personal property, whether or not heritable or moveable, and includes money and choses in action and any other intangible or incorporeal property;

---

[1] OJ L214, 4.8.2006, p.29.

"terrorist financing" means an offence under section 13 of the Criminal Justice (Terrorist Offences) Act 2005;

"Third Money Laundering Directive" means Directive 2005/60/EC of the European Parliament and of the Council of 26 October 2005 on the prevention of the use of the financial system for the purpose of money laundering and terrorist financing,[2] as amended by the following:

(a) Directive 2007/64/EC of the European Parliament and of the Council of 13 November 2007 on payment services in the internal market amending Directives 97/7/EC, 2002/65/EC, 2005/60/EC and 2006/48/EC and repealing Directive 97/5/EC;[3]

(b) Directive 2009/110/EC of the European Parliament and of the Council of 16 September 2009 on the taking up, pursuit and prudential supervision of the business of electronic money institutions amending Directives 2005/60/EC and 2006/48/EC and repealing Directive 2000/46/EC.[4]

(2) A word or expression used in this Act and also in the Third Money Laundering Directive or the Implementing Directive has, unless the contrary intention appears, the same meaning in this Act as in that Directive.

Section Note

The effect of s.2(2) is that anyone reading the Act must also consult the measures to which it cross-refers. It is perhaps to be regretted that the Oireachtas has never seen fit to establish a single dictionary or glossary of terms separate from the enactments it passes so that a person coming to legislation can have regard to that dictionary or glossary instead of cross-referring into legislation that often cross-refers into still further legislation. Appendix 1 of this text indicates the various terms defined respectively in the Act, the Directive and the Implementing Directive and the measure/provision in which the relevant definition is found. Certain of the terms defined in s.2(1) are considered further below.

"Minister"

Since the enactment of the Act, the title of the Minister has been changed to "Minister for Justice and Law Reform" (and his Department has been re-named as the "Department of Justice and Law Reform") by the Justice, Equality and Law Reform (Alteration of Name of Department and Title of Minister) Order 2010 (S.I. No. 216 of 2010). In this text the term "Minister for Justice and Law Reform" is used to refer to the Minister except when referring to the Minister in the context of the Oireachtas debates that preceded the enactment of the Act, at which the then-titled "Minister for Justice, Equality and Law Reform" generally attended.

---

[2] OJ L309, 25.11.2005, p.15.
[3] OJ L319, 5.12.2007, p.1.
[4] OJ L267, 10.10.2009, p.7.

"[T]errorist financing"

The term "terrorist financing" is defined as meaning an offence under s.13 of the Criminal Justice (Terrorist Offences) Act 2005. The 2005 Act gives effect to a number of international instruments directed at terrorism and enabled (and enables) Ireland to meet commitments which it has undertaken as part of the European Union and the broader international community, including commitments arising from United Nations Security Resolution 1373 (adopted in response to the 9/11 attack on the United States). The 2005 Act also amended Ireland's law more generally so as to enhance Ireland's capacity to address the problem of international terrorism, provides for the retention of communications data, and amends the European Arrest Warrant Act 2003. Pt.4 of the 2005 Act makes specific provision as regards the suppression of the financing of terrorism. Broadly, the term "terrorist financing", as defined in the 2005 Act, comprises what the colloquial term would suggest, *i.e.* providing, collecting or receiving funds that will be used to carry out terrorist acts or for the benefit or for the benefit or purposes of a terrorist group. Specifically, s.13 provides that a person is guilty of financing terrorism if: (1) in or outside Ireland, the person by any means, directly or indirectly, unlawfully and wilfully provides, collects or receives funds intending that they be used or knowing that they will be used, in whole or in part in order to carry out (a) an act that constitutes an offence under the law of Ireland and within the scope of, and as defined in, any treaty that is listed in the annex to the Terrorist Financing Convention, or (b) an act (other than one referred to in (a)) that is intended to cause death or serious bodily injury to a civilian or to any other person not taking an active part in the hostilities in a situation of armed conflict, and the purpose of which is, by its nature or context, to intimidate a population or to compel a government or an international organisation to do or abstain from doing any act; or (2) the person by any means, directly or indirectly, unlawfully and wilfully provides, collects or receives funds intending that they be used or knowing that they will be used, in whole or in part (a) for the benefit or purposes of a terrorist group as defined in s.4 of the 2005 Act, or (b) in order to carry out an act (other than one referred to in (a) or (b) above that is an offence under s.6 of the 2005 Act. (A person who attempts to commit either of these offences is likewise guilty of an offence (per s.13(2) and (4) of the 2005 Act)).

The term "Terrorist Financing Convention" refers to the International Convention for the Suppression of the Financing of Terrorism adapted by resolution 54/109 of the General Assembly of the United Nations on 9 December 1999, which entered into force against Ireland on 30 July 2005 (see Treaty Series 2006, No. 10). The term "terrorist group" has the meaning given that term in Art.2 of the Council Framework Decision of 13 June 2002 on combating terrorism (O.J. L164, 22.6.2002, p.3) *i.e.* "a structured group of more than two persons, established over a period of time and acting in concert to commit terrorist offences"; the term "structured group", per Art.2 of the Council

Framework Decision, means "a group that is not randomly formed for the immediate commission of an offence and that does not need to have formally defined roles for its members, continuity of its member-ship or a developed structure.". S.6 of the 2005 Act establishes various terrorist offences, including engaging in a "terrorist activity" or "terrorist-linked activity", attempting to engage in same, or making a threat to engage in a terrorist activity, the quoted terms being defined in s.4 of the 2005 Act.

As mentioned in the preface to this text, as with other organised criminal groups a terrorist group's income may be derived from crimes such as kidnapping, extortion, smuggling, fraud, theft, drug trafficking, *etc.* and the laundering of the proceeds of those crimes could reasonably be expected to be caught by the anti-money laundering régime. However, there are aspects of terrorist financing that would not constitute money laundering. For example, fundraising activities may be carried out in the name of charitable or relief organisations that are the front for a terrorist group. This fundraising could include collection of subscriptions, sale of publications, speaking tours, cultural and social events, door-to-door solicitation, appeals for funds to wealthy donors and donations by persons of a portion of their earnings to a particular group. In short, whereas money laundering is concerned with "dirty money", terrorist financing can also involve "clean money". Terrorist financing can also involve relatively small sums of money. The Guidance Notes on the 2005 Act published under the auspices of The Money Laundering Steering Committee helpfully outline an array of financial transactions whose characteristics may prompt further scrutiny from an anti-terrorist financing perspective (see The Money Laundering Steering Committee, "Guidance on the Offence of Finan-cing Terrorism and the Financial Sanctions Regime for Bodies Designated under Section 32 of the Criminal Justice Act, 1994" (Dublin: 2005)). For an account of some of the implications of the 2005 Act for solicitors, see Barrett, M., "Shadow of a gunman", (2005) 99(5) *Law Society Gazette*, 14.

Regulations

3.—(1) The Minister may, after consulting with the Minister for Finance, by regulations provide for any matter referred to in this Act as prescribed or to be prescribed.

(2) Regulations under this Act may contain such incidental, supple-mentary and consequential provisions as appear to the Minister to be necessary or expedient for the purposes of the regulations.

(3) Every regulation made under this Act shall be laid before each House of the Oireachtas as soon as may be after it is made and, if a resolution annulling the regulation is passed by either such House within the next 21 days on which that House has sat after the regulation is laid

before it, the regulation shall be annulled accordingly, but without prejudice to the validity of anything previously done under the regulation.

Section Note

A list of the regulations made under the Act and extant at the time of writing is set out elsewhere above.

Repeals and revocations

4.—(1) Sections 31, 32, 32A, 57(1) to (6) and (7)(*a*), 57A and 58(2) of the Criminal Justice Act 1994 are repealed.

(2) The statutory instruments specified in *column (1)* of *Schedule 1* are revoked to the extent specified in *column (3)* of that Schedule.

Section Note

Section 4(1) repeals various provisions of the Criminal Justice Act 1994 that were concerned with money laundering. Section 31 of that Act established the offence of money laundering. S.32 identified the various persons who constituted designated bodies for the purposes of the Act and established customer due diligence obligations for such persons. Section 32A made clear that references to an offence in Pt.IV of the 1994 Act (the Part concerned with money laundering) included Revenue offences. (s.32A is of relatively recent provenance, having itself been inserted into the 1994 Act by s.105(e) of the Criminal Justice (Mutual Assistance) Act 2008). S.57(1) to (6) and 7(a) was concerned with reporting obligations. Section 57A empowered the Minister to designate places that in his opinion did not have adequate procedures for the detection of money laundering and required, *inter alia*, designated bodies to report to the Garda Síochána any transaction connected with such a place. Section 58(2) established the offence of tipping-off in respect of reports made under s.57.

Expenses

5.—The expenses incurred by the Minister in the administration of this Act shall, to such extent as may be sanctioned by the Minister for Finance, be paid out of moneys provided by the Oireachtas and the expenses incurred by the Minister for Finance in the administration of this Act shall be paid out of moneys provided by the Oireachtas.

PART 2

Money Laundering Offences

Interpretation (*Part 2*)

6.—In this Part—
"criminal conduct" means—

(*a*) conduct that constitutes an offence, or

(*b*) conduct occurring in a place outside the State that constitutes an offence under the law of the place and would constitute an offence if it were to occur in the State;

"proceeds of criminal conduct" means any property that is derived from or obtained through criminal conduct, whether directly or indirectly, or in whole or in part, and whether that criminal conduct occurs before, on or after the commencement of this Part.

Section Note

"criminal conduct"

The definition of "criminal conduct" is consistent with the first of the FATF 40 Recommendations which states, *inter alia*, that:

> "Predicate offences for money laundering should extend to conduct that occurred in another country, which constitutes an offence in that country, and which would have constituted a predicate offence had it occurred domestically. Countries may provide that the only prerequisite is that the conduct would have constituted a predicate offence had it occurred domestically." (FATF, *FATF 40 Recommendations*, p.3).

(Section 16 of the Act provides, for the avoidance of doubt, that any reference in Pt.2 to an offence under the law of a place outside Ireland includes a reference to a Revenue offence). Notably, it is not necessary that the criminal conduct of which the "proceeds of criminal conduct" are proceeds be criminal conduct of a particular gravity. Again, this is consistent with the first of the FATF 40 Recommendations, though the provisions of the Act in this regard are at the more stringent end of what the first recommendation anticipates. Per the first of the FATF 40 Recommendations:

> "Countries should apply the crime of money laundering to all serious offences, with a view to including the widest range of predicate offences. Predicate offences may be described by reference to all offences, or to a threshold linked either to a category of serious offences or to the penalty of imprisonment applicable to the predicate offence." (FATF, *FATF 40 Recommendations*, p.3).

Ireland has elected to make all offences capable of constituting an offence on which the crime of money laundering may be predicated.

"proceeds of criminal conduct"

The term "proceeds of criminal conduct" is comprehensive, embracing any property that is derived from or obtained through criminal conduct. When applied to tax evasion the definition may present a logical difficulty. Suppose, for example, that a man earns his income legitimately but decides not to declare that income for tax purposes. This is reprehensible behaviour but none of the monies that he earns derives from criminal conduct and thus an argument could perhaps be made that none of those monies are the "proceeds" of criminal conduct. That said, the fact that reports made pursuant to Ch.4 of the Act must be made to the Garda Síochána and also to the Revenue Commissioners perhaps suggests that, regardless of any (if any) logical difficulties that may arise, the Oireachtas considers undeclared income to represent, at least in part, the "proceeds of criminal conduct" notwithstanding that the part which constitutes such proceeds may be difficult to identify. What constitute the "proceeds of criminal conduct" is given further attention in the consideration of s.11 of the Act below.

Money laundering occurring in State

7.—(1) A person commits an offence if—

(a) the person engages in any of the following acts in relation to property that is the proceeds of criminal conduct:
  (i) concealing or disguising the true nature, source, location, disposition, movement or ownership of the property, or any rights relating to the property;
  (ii) converting, transferring, handling, acquiring, possessing or using the property;
  (iii) removing the property from, or bringing the property into, the State, and

(b) the person knows or believes (or is reckless as to whether or not) the property is the proceeds of criminal conduct.

(2) A person who attempts to commit an offence under *subsection (1)* commits an offence.

(3) A person who commits an offence under this section is liable—

(a) on summary conviction, to a fine not exceeding €5,000 or imprisonment for a term not exceeding 12 months (or both), or
(b) on conviction on indictment, to a fine or imprisonment for a term not exceeding 14 years (or both).

(4) A reference in this section to knowing or believing that property is the proceeds of criminal conduct includes a reference to knowing or

believing that the property probably comprises the proceeds of criminal conduct.

(5) For the purposes of *subsections (1)* and *(2)*, a person is reckless as to whether or not property is the proceeds of criminal conduct if the person disregards, in relation to property, a risk of such a nature and degree that, considering the circumstances in which the person carries out any act referred to in *subsection (1)* or *(2)*, the disregard of that risk involves culpability of a high degree.

(6) For the purposes of *subsections (1)* and *(2)*, a person handles property if the person—

(*a*) receives, or arranges to receive, the property, or

(*b*) retains, removes, disposes of or realises the property, or arranges to do any of those things, for the benefit of another person.

(7) A person does not commit an offence under this section in relation to the doing of any thing in relation to property that is the proceeds of criminal conduct so long as—

(*a*) the person does the thing in accordance with a direction, order or authorisation given under *Part 3,* or

(*b*) without prejudice to the generality of *paragraph (a)*, the person is a designated person, within the meaning of *Part 4,* who makes a report in relation to the property, and does the thing, in accordance with *section 42*.

Money laundering outside State in certain circumstances

8.—(1) A person who, in a place outside the State, engages in conduct that would, if the conduct occurred in the State, constitute an offence under *section 7* commits an offence if any of the following circumstances apply:

(*a*) the conduct takes place on board an Irish ship, within the meaning of section 9 of the Mercantile Marine Act 1955,

(*b*) the conduct takes place on an aircraft registered in the State,

(*c*) the conduct constitutes an offence under the law of that place and the person is—

(i) an individual who is a citizen of Ireland or ordinarily resident in the State, or

(ii) a body corporate established under the law of the State or a company registered under the Companies Acts,

(*d*) a request for the person's surrender, for the purpose of trying him or her for an offence in respect of the conduct, has been made under Part II of the Extradition Act 1965 by any country and the request has been finally refused (whether or not as a result of a decision of a court), or

(*e*) a European arrest warrant has been received from an issuing state for the purpose of bringing proceedings against the person for an offence in respect of the conduct, and a final determination has been made that—

(i) the European arrest warrant should not be endorsed for execution in the State under the European Arrest Warrant Act 2003, or

(ii) the person should not be surrendered to the issuing state.

(2) A person who commits an offence under this section is liable—

(*a*) on summary conviction, to a fine not exceeding €5,000 or imprisonment for a term not exceeding 12 months (or both), or

(*b*) on conviction on indictment, to a fine or imprisonment for a term not exceeding 14 years (or both).

(3) A person who has his or her principal residence in the State for the 12 months immediately preceding the commission of an offence under this section is, in a case where *subsection (1)(c)* applies, taken to be ordinarily resident in the State on the date of the commission of the offence.

(4) In this section, "European arrest warrant" and "issuing state" have the same meanings as they have in the European Arrest Warrant Act 2003.

Section Note

Offence of money laundering occurring in Ireland

Sections 7 and 8 respectively establish, for the purposes of Irish law, the offence of money laundering where it occurs (a) in Ireland and (b) outside Ireland (in a number of prescribed circumstances). To commit the offence of money laundering in Ireland, a person must engage in any of various acts in relation to property that is the proceeds of criminal conduct. It will be recalled that the terms "property" and "proceeds of criminal conduct" are defined respectively in ss.2(1) and 6 of the Act. (The term "property" is also defined in Art.3(3) of the Directive. Though the respective definitions of this term in the Act and the Directive do not precisely tally, offhand the difference between them does not appear to be of practical significance).

Section 7, like various other provisions throughout the Act makes it an offence for a "person" to engage in certain acts. The term "person" is not defined in the Act. However, s.18 of the Interpretation Act 2005 (No. 23 of 2005) provides in this regard that the term "person" should be read "as importing a body corporate (whether a corporation aggregate or a corporation sole) and an unincorporated body of persons, as well as an individual, and the subsequent use of any pronoun in place of a further use of "person" shall be read accordingly". This definition of "person" is consistent with the second limb of the second FATF Recommendation which requires that, without prejudice to the criminal liability of individuals (natural persons), liability should extend to legal persons. Thus, per the FATF Recommendations:

"Criminal liability, and, where that is not possible, civil or administrative liability, should apply to legal persons….Legal persons should be subject to effective, proportionate and dissuasive sanctions. Such measures should be without prejudice to the criminal liability of individuals." (FATF, *FATF 40 Recommendations*, p.4).

Basic elements of s.7 offences

There are two basic elements to the offence established by s.7(1). First, the person must engage in one or more defined acts in relation to property that is the proceeds of criminal conduct. Second, the person must know or believe (or be reckless as to whether or not) that property is the proceeds of criminal conduct. An attempt to commit a s.7(1) offence is, per s.7(2), itself an offence (as will be seen in the consideration of s.9 of the Act, it is also an offence under s.9(1) of the Act for a person to attempt, in a place outside Ireland, to commit an offence under s.7(1)). Of interest in this regard is the *mens rea* requirement for the crime of money laundering, namely that it can in effect be proven where a person believes the property is probably the proceeds of crime. A number of clarifying provisions (s.7(4) to (6)) supplement these other provisions. Section 7(5) of the Act provides a definition as to what constitutes being "reckless" as to whether or not property is the proceeds of criminal conduct for the purposes of s.7(1) and (2), in effect requiring that a person who carries out one of the defined acts referred to in s.7(1) in relation to property be guilty of "culpability of a high degree" in disregarding a particular risk.

Non-liability

Section 7(7) is one of a number of provisions in the Act that exempt a person from a liability that would otherwise arise under the Act. These various provisions are considered below.

A. Not money laundering

Section 7(7) has the effect that a person does not commit an offence under s.7(1) by doing anything in relation to property that is the proceeds of criminal conduct if any of four circumstances apply: (1) the person does the thing in accordance with a direction given by a member of the Garda Síochána not below the rank of superintendent, pursuant to s.17(1) of the Act, not to carry out a specified service or transaction; (2) the person does the thing in accordance with a District Court order made pursuant to Pt.3 of the Act; (3) the person does the thing in accordance with an authorisation under s.23(1) of the Act, under which, in certain circumstances, a member of the Garda Síochána not below the rank of superintendent may authorise a person to do a thing referred to in s.7(1); or (4) the person is a designated person required to make a report to the Garda Síochána and the Revenue Commissioners under s.42 and (s.7(7) is not specific in this regard but it would appear that it is referring to the circumstances anticipated in s.42(7)) the designated person, prior to the sending of the report, proceeds with a suspicious transaction or service connected with the said report (or with a transaction or service the subject of the report) where (a) the limited circumstances identified in s.42(7) apply and (b) (consistent with s.42(8)) there is no current Garda direction or District Court order prohibiting the designated person from so proceeding.

B. No breach of any requirement/restriction imposed by
an enactment or rule of law
Section 17(6) of the Act provides that an act or omission in compliance with a Garda direction or District Court order made under s.17:

> "shall not be treated, for any purpose, as a breach of any requirement or restriction imposed by any other enactment or rule of law".

Section 23(2) of the Act provides that the doing of anything (though not it seems the omitting from doing anything) in accordance with a Garda authorisation under s.23 likewise

> "shall not be treated, for any purpose, as a breach of any requirement or restriction imposed by any other enactment or rule of law".

(It is presumably the reference to "any other enactment" in s.23(2) that prompted the inclusion in the Act of s.23(3) so as to make clear that the exception from liability granted by s.23(2) is without prejudice to the exception from liability under s.7 of the Act granted by s.7(7)).

Section 47 of the Act provides that the disclosure of information by a person in accordance with Ch.4 of Pt.4 (which establishes the reporting obligations under the Act):

> "shall not be treated, for any purpose as a breach of any restriction imposed by any other enactment or rule of law on disclosure by the person or any other person on whose behalf the disclosure is made".

Section 83(1) of the Act provides that the disclosure or production of information by a person in accordance with Ch.8 of Pt.4 (which is largely concerned with the powers and responsibilities of competent authorities and particularly State competent authorities):

> "shall not be treated as a breach of any restriction under any enactment or rule of law on disclosure or production by the person or any other person on whose behalf the information or document is disclosed or produced".

(Nor does the production of any item in accordance with Ch.8 prejudice any lien claimed over same (see s.83(2)).

Section 112 of the Act provides that a disclosure in good faith to a member of the Garda Síochána or to any person who is concerned in the investigation or financing of an offence of money laundering or terrorist financing of (a) a suspicion that any property has been obtained in connection with any such offence or derives from property so obtained, or (b) any matter on which such a suspicion is based:

> "shall not be treated, for any purpose, as a breach of any restriction on the disclosure of information imposed by any other enactment or rule of law."

When juxtaposed together as above, both the similarities and the differences between these various provisions becomes more apparent. Thus, for example, ss. 17(6) and 23(2) apply to a breach of any requirement or restriction; ss. 47, 83(1) and 112 apply to a breach of any restriction only. Sections 17(6), 23(2), 47 and 112 refer to a breach under any other enactment (*i.e.* other than the Act) or rule of law; s.83(1) refers to a breach under any enactment (including the Act) or rule of law. Sections 17(6) and 23(2) both refer to any requirement or restriction; ss. 47, 83(1) and 112 refer only to a specific form of restriction.

Penalties

Consistent with the seventeenth of the FATF 40 Recommendations (which recommends that countries have effective, proportionate and dissuasive sanctions for persons who fail to comply with anti-money laundering or terrorist financing obligations (see FATF, *FATF 40 Recommendations*, p.9)), stringent penalties are prescribed by s.7(3) of the Act for a person who commits an offence under s.7. These penalties are marginally more stringent than the penalties that pertained under the now repealed s.31(2)(a) of the Criminal Justice Act 1994 — which provided for a maximum fine on summary conviction of €1,904.61 — but otherwise imposed penalties identical to those now pertaining under s.7. Even so, it was suggested during the debates which preceded the enactment of the Act that the penalties arising under s.7 are not stringent enough. Indeed one member of the Dáil suggested, during that House's Second Stage reading of the Bill, that the maximum penalties applicable upon conviction were so light that they could conceivably give an incentive to persons minded to conduct money laundering. Thus, per Deputy Bernard J. Durkan:

> "I can assure the Minister that the threat of 12 months' imprisonment or a fine of €5,000 is of no significance to people in that bracket. It could become an incentive. After all, if the value of the moneys to be laundered is sufficiently high, it would be good value to spend 21 months in prison and be fined €5,000. Do we really believe a term of imprisonment of 12 to 14 years will deter somebody who has the opportunity to launder €10 million or €15 million or, as in many cases, considerably more? I do not regard

this sentence as long enough to deter people from laundering such sums – it might even encourage them." 695(2) *Díospóir-eachtaí Parlaiminte* (19.11.2009), 276.

Appendix 2 of this text identifies all of the various offences arising under the Act and the prescribed penalties for same.

There is of course a civil law dimension to money laundering also, in that, for example, a bank engaged in money laundering could be held liable to account for the proceeds of crime to the victim of the fraud under the doctrine of constructive trusteeship assuming there is a victim — and not all crimes involve someone who would be a "victim" in the classic sense, *e.g* drug dealing. This civil law dimension to money laundering is not addressed in the Act and thus falls outside the scope of this text (see further on the issue of civil liability in this regard, Breslin, J. *Banking Law*, 2nd edition (Dublin, 2007), pp. 76ff).

Offence of money laundering outside Ireland
Section 8 makes it an offence for the purposes of Irish law where, in defined instances, a person in a place outside Ireland engages in conduct that would constitute an offence under s.7 of the Act if that conduct occurred in Ireland. (See further the table of offences arising under the Act (and the penalties for same) in Appendix 2 of this text).

The term "Irish ship", as employed in s.8(1)(a), is deemed to have the meaning given that term in s.9 of the Mercantile Marine Act 1955. Section 9 of the Mercantile Marine Act 1955 provides that the following ships constitute Irish ships for the purposes of that Act: ships wholly owned by the Government of Ireland or a Minister of State; ships wholly owned by (a) Irish citizens or (b) Irish corporate entities and which are not registered under the law of another country; and other ships registered or deemed to be registered under the 1955 Act.

The terms "European arrest warrant" and "issuing state" (as employed in s.8(1)(e) of the Act) are given the meanings afforded those terms in the European Arrest Warrant Act 2003. As defined in the European Arrest Warrant Act 2003, the term "European arrest warrant" means, per s.2(1) of that Act, a warrant, order or decision of a judicial authority of a "Member State" (*i.e.* an EU Member State, other than Ireland, or Gibraltar) issued under such laws as give effect in that State to the Council Framework Decision of 13 June 2002 on the European arrest warrant and the surrender procedures between Member States (O.J. L.190, 18.7.2002, p.1), for the arrest and surrender by Ireland to that Member State of a person in respect of an offence committed or alleged to have been committed by him or her under the law of that Member State. The term "issuing state", again per s.2(1) of the 2003 Act, means, in relation to a European arrest warrant, a Member State designated by the Minister for Foreign Affairs as having, under its national law, given effect to the above-mentioned

Council Framework Decision, a judicial authority of which has issued that European arrest warrant.

Attempts, outside State, to commit offence in State

9.—(1) A person who attempts, in a place outside the State, to commit an offence under *section 7(1)* is guilty of an offence.

(2) A person who commits an offence under this section is liable—

(*a*) on summary conviction, to a fine not exceeding €5,000 or imprisonment for a term not exceeding 12 months (or both), or

(*b*) on conviction on indictment, to a fine or imprisonment for a term not exceeding 14 years (or both).

Section Note

An attempt to commit a s.7(1) offence is, per s.7(2), itself an offence. In a related vein, it is an offence under s.9(1) of the Act for a person to attempt, in a place outside Ireland, to commit an offence under s.7(1). See further the table of offences arising under the Act (and the penalties for same) in Appendix 2 of this text.

Aiding, abetting, counselling or procuring outside State commission of offence in State

10.—(1) A person who, in a place outside the State, aids, abets, counsels or procures the commission of an offence under *section 7* is guilty of an offence.

(2) A person who commits an offence under this section is liable—

(*a*) on summary conviction, to a fine not exceeding €5,000 or imprisonment for a term not exceeding 12 months (or both), or

(*b*) on conviction on indictment, to a fine or imprisonment for a term not exceeding 14 years (or both).

(3) This section is without prejudice to section 7(1) of the Criminal Law Act 1997.

Section Note

Section 10 continues in the extra-jurisdictional vein commenced in s.8 and continued in s.9. Section 8, it will be recalled, is concerned with money-laundering outside Ireland. Section 9 is concerned with attempts outside Ireland to commit an offence within Ireland. Section 10 makes it an offence for a person in a place outside Ireland to aid, abet, counsel or procure the commission of a s.7 offence. The same punishments as arise for s.7, 8 and 9 offences also pertain in respect of an offence under s.10. Section 10(3) states that s.10 is without prejudice to s.7(1) of the Criminal Law Act 1997. That last provision is concerned with penalties for assisting offenders. See further the table of offences arising under the Act (and the penalties for same) in Appendix 2 of this text.

Presumptions and other matters

11.—(1) In this section "specified conduct" means any of the following acts referred to in *section 7(1)* (including *section 7(1)* as applied by *section 8* or *9*):

(*a*) concealing or disguising the true nature, source, location, disposition, movement or ownership of property, or any rights relating to property;

(*b*) converting, transferring, handling, acquiring, possessing or using property;

(*c*) removing property from, or bringing property into, the State or a place outside the State.

(2) In proceedings for an offence under *section 7, 8* or *9*, where an accused has engaged, or attempted to engage, in specified conduct in relation to property that is the proceeds of criminal conduct, in circumstances in which it is reasonable to conclude that the accused—

(*a*) knew or believed the property was the proceeds of criminal conduct, or

(*b*) was reckless as to whether or not the property was the proceeds of criminal conduct,

the accused is presumed to have so known or believed, or been so reckless, unless the court or jury, as the case may be, is satisfied, having regard to the whole of the evidence, that there is a reasonable doubt that the accused so knew or believed or was so reckless.

(3) In proceedings for an offence under *section 7, 8* or *9*, where an accused has engaged in, or attempted to engage in, specified conduct in relation to property in circumstances in which it is reasonable to conclude that the property is the proceeds of criminal conduct, those circumstances are evidence that the property is the proceeds of criminal conduct.

(4) For the purposes of *subsection (3)*, circumstances in which it is reasonable to conclude that property is the proceeds of criminal conduct include any of the following:

(*a*) the value of the property concerned is, it is reasonable to conclude, out of proportion to the income and expenditure of the accused or another person in a case where the accused engaged in the specified conduct concerned on behalf of, or at the request of, the other person;

(*b*) the specified conduct concerned involves the actual or purported purchase or sale of goods or services for an amount that is, it is reasonable to conclude, out of proportion to the market value of the goods or services (whether the amount represents an overvaluation or an undervaluation);

(*c*) the specified conduct concerned involves one or more transactions using false names;

(*d*) the accused has stated that he or she engaged in the specified conduct concerned on behalf of, or at the request of, another person and has not provided information to the Garda Síochána enabling the other person to be identified and located;

(*e*) where an accused has concealed or disguised the true nature, source, location, disposition, movement or ownership of the property, or any rights relating to the property, the accused has no reasonable explanation for that concealment or disguise.

(5) Nothing in *subsection (4)* limits the circumstances in which it is reasonable to conclude, for the purposes of *subsection (3)*, that property is the proceeds of criminal conduct.

(6) Nothing in this section prevents *subsections (2)* and *(3)* being applied in the same proceedings.

(7) *Subsections (2)* to *(6)* extend to proceedings for an offence under—

(*a*) *section 10*, or

(*b*) section 7(1) of the Criminal Law Act 1997 of aiding, abetting, counselling or procuring the commission of an offence under *section 7, 8* or *9*, and for that purpose any reference to an accused in *subsections (2)* to *(6)* is to be construed as a reference to a person who committed, or is alleged to have committed, the offence concerned.

(8) In proceedings for an offence under this Part, or an offence under section 7(1) of the Criminal Law Act 1997 referred to in *subsection (7)(b)*, it is not necessary, in order to prove that property is the proceeds of criminal conduct, to establish that—

(*a*) a particular offence or a particular class of offence comprising criminal conduct was committed in relation to the property, or

(*b*) a particular person committed an offence comprising criminal conduct in relation to the property.

(9) In proceedings for an offence under this Part, or an offence under section 7(1) of the Criminal Law Act 1997 referred to in *subsection (7)(b)*, it is not a defence for the accused to show that the accused believed the property concerned to be the proceeds of a particular offence comprising criminal conduct when in fact the property was the proceeds of another offence.

Section Note

Section 11 amplifies on certain matters concerning the "proceeds of criminal conduct" (as defined in s.6). Section 11(1) commences by defining certain conduct done in relation to property as "specified conduct" for the purposes of s.11. Section 11(2) and (3) then make certain provision as regards proceedings for an offence under s.7, 8 or 9 of the Act where an accused has engaged, or attempted to engage, in specified conduct in relation to property that is the proceeds of criminal conduct. Section 11(2) establishes a rebuttable presumption that an accused may be presumed to have known or believed that (or been reckless as to whether or not) property was the proceeds of criminal conduct in circumstances in which it is reasonable to conclude that an accused so knew or believed or was reckless. Section 11(3) provides that in proceedings for an offence under 7, 8 or 9, where specified conduct is engaged in, or attempted to be engaged in, in relation property in circumstances in which it is "reasonable" to conclude that the property is the proceeds of criminal conduct, those circumstances are evidence that the property is the proceeds of criminal conduct. A question that immediately arises out of s.11(3) is in what circumstances it is "reasonable" to conclude that property is the proceeds of criminal conduct? Section 11(4) gives some examples in which it is reasonable so to conclude. Unfortunately the first two examples given themselves include a reference to reasonableness and thus it is questionable as to how helpful they are by way of examples. Thus, s.11(4)(a) and (b) between them provide that where the value of property is "it is reasonable to conclude" not proportionate to the income and expenditure of the accused (or another person on whose behalf or at whose request the specified conduct is done) or where the amount paid on the actual or purported purchase or sale of goods or services is "it is reasonable to conclude" out of proportion to their market value, then it would be reasonable to conclude that particular property is the proceeds of criminal conduct. This merely converts the question as to when it is reasonable to conclude that property is the proceeds of criminal conduct into a question as to when it is reasonable to conclude as indicated in s.11(4)(a) and (b). Section 11(4)(c) and (d) give more straightforward examples of circumstances in which not only is it reasonable to conclude that property is the proceeds of criminal conduct but also there is no additional reasonableness criterion to which one must have regard as in s.11(4)(a) and (b). However, s.11(4)(e) returns to the form of s.11(4)(a) and (b) indicating that where an accused has no reasonable explanation for certain concealment or disguise of property or rights relating thereto then it is reasonable to conclude that the relevant property is the proceeds of criminal conduct. This merely converts the question as to when it is reasonable to conclude that property is the proceeds of criminal conduct into a question as to whether an accused has a reasonable explanation for a particular concealment or disguise.

Section 11(5) and (6) make certain incidental provision to the preceding provisions of s.11. Section 11(7) to (9) between them make certain provision applicable *inter alia* to proceedings arising under Pt.2 of the Act, s.10 of the Act and also certain proceedings arising under the Criminal Law Act 1997. (That earlier Act provides *inter alia* for the abolition of the distinction between a felony and a misdemeanour, the abolition of penal servitude, hard labour, prison divisions and corporal punishment and makes certain related provision). Section 11(8) provides that in the circumstances in which it applies it is not necessary, in order to prove that property is the proceeds of criminal conduct, to establish that (a) a particular offence or a particular class of offence comprising criminal conduct was committed in relation to the property, or (b) a particular person committed an offence comprising criminal conduct in relation to the property. In short, so long as property is the "proceeds of criminal conduct" it is possible to be guilty of an offence, *inter alia* under Pt.2 of the Act, in relation to those proceeds of criminal conduct regardless of the nature of the offence that renders that property the proceeds of criminal conduct and without any need to prove who committed the primary offence that renders particular property the proceeds of criminal conduct. Section 11(9) provides that in the circumstances in which it applies it is not a defence to show that an accused believed certain property to be the proceeds of Offence A when in fact it was the proceeds of Offence B.

Location of proceedings relating to offences committed outside State

12.—Proceedings for an offence under *section 8, 9* or *10* may be taken in any place in the State and the offence may for all incidental purposes be treated as having been committed in that place.

Section Note

It will be recalled that ss.8, 9 and 10 of the Act are concerned respectively with money laundering outside Ireland in certain circumstances, attempts outside Ireland to commit an offence inside Ireland and aiding, abetting, counselling or procuring outside Ireland the commission of an offence in Ireland. Section 12 makes provision as regards where in Ireland proceedings for any such offence may be brought and related provision as to where the relevant offence should be treated as having been committed.

Consent of DPP required for proceedings for offences committed outside State

13.—If a person is charged with an offence under *section 8, 9* or *10*, no further proceedings in the matter (other than any remand in custody or on bail) may be taken except by, or with the consent of, the Director of Public Prosecutions.

Certificate may be evidence in proceedings under this Part

14.—(1) In any proceedings for an offence under this Part in which it is alleged that property the subject of the offence is the proceeds of criminal conduct occurring in a place outside the State, a certificate—

(*a*) purporting to be signed by a lawyer practising in the place, and
(*b*) stating that such conduct is an offence in that place, is evidence of the matters referred to in that certificate, unless the contrary is shown.

(2) A certificate referred to in *subsection (1)* is taken to have been signed by the person purporting to have signed it, unless the contrary is shown.

(3) In a case where a certificate referred to in *subsection (1)* is written in a language other than the Irish language or the English language, unless the contrary is shown—

(*a*) a document purporting to be a translation of that certificate into the Irish language or the English language, as the case may be, and that is certified as correct by a person appearing to be competent to so certify, is taken—

(i) to be a correct translation of the certificate, and

(ii) to have been certified by the person purporting to have certified it, and

(*b*) the person is taken to be competent to so certify.

(4) In any proceedings for an offence under *section 8* committed in the circumstances referred to in *section 8(1)(c),* a certificate purporting to be signed by an officer of the Department of Foreign Affairs and stating that—

(*a*) a passport was issued by that Department to a person on a specified date, and

(*b*) to the best of the officer's knowledge and belief, the person has not ceased to be an Irish citizen, is evidence that the person was an Irish citizen on the date on which the offence is alleged to have been committed, and is taken to have been signed by the person purporting to have signed it, unless the contrary is shown.

(5) In any proceedings for an offence under *section 8* committed in the circumstances referred to in *section 8(1)(d)* or *(e),* a certificate purporting to be signed by the Minister and stating any of the matters referred to in that paragraph is evidence of those matters, and is taken to have been signed by the Minister, unless the contrary is shown.

Double jeopardy

15.—A person who has been acquitted or convicted of an offence in a place outside the State shall not be proceeded against for an offence under *section 8, 9* or *10* consisting of the conduct, or substantially the same conduct, that constituted the offence of which the person has been acquitted or convicted.

Revenue offence committed outside State

16.—For the avoidance of doubt, a reference in this Part to an offence under the law of a place outside the State includes a reference to an offence in connection with taxes, duties, customs or exchange regulation.

PART 3

Directions, Orders and Authorisations Relating to Investigations

General Note

Section 17(1) empowers a member of the Garda Síochána not below the rank of superintendent to direct a person in writing not to carry out a specified service or transaction for a period of not more than seven days in defined instances. Section 17(2) empowers a District Court judge to make a similar order, upon application by a member of the Garda Síochána, subject to a 28-day maximum. Failure to comply with such a direction or order is an offence (per s.17(5)). (See further the table of offences arising under the Act (and the penalties for same) in Appendix 2 of this text). Section 17(6), considered in the context of s.7(7) above, grants a certain exception from liability to a person acting in compliance with a direction or order under s.17. Section 18 requires that any person affected by the direction or order be given written notice of same as soon as practicable after a direction/order is given/ made, save in defined instances. Section 19 empowers a judge of the District Court, in particular circumstances, to revoke a direction or order while it is in force on the application of the person affected thereby. In a not dissimilar vein s.20 empowers a District Court judge, in particular circumstances, to make any order of a defined type in relation to property that is the subject of a direction or order. Under s.21(1) of the Act, a s.17 direction or order ceases to have effect upon the cessation an investigation into whether the service or transaction the subject of the direction or order would, if done, comprise, or assist in, money laundering or terrorist financing. As soon as practicable thereafter a member of the Garda Síochána must give written notice of the cessation to the person to whom the direction/order has been given, and any other person who that member of the Garda Síochána is aware is affected by the order (per s.21(2)). (Whereas, under s.18(1), notice of a direction or order under s.17 must be given by the member of the Garda Síochána who gave the direction or applied for the order any member of the Garda Síochána may give the notice referred to in s.18(2) and s.21(2)). Section 22 of the Act affords a degree of protection to persons making report under Ch.4 of Pt.4, prohibiting disclosure of such report (though not perhaps the fact that the report exists) to the relevant District Court judge. Under s.23(1) a member of the Garda Síochána not below the rank of superintendent may, by written notice, authorise a person to do a thing referred to in s.7(1), the provision that establishes the offence of money laundering occurring in Ireland, if that member is satisfied that the thing is necessary for the purposes of an investigation into an offence. In short, a member of the Gardaí can authorise what would otherwise be wrongdoing where that is necessary for the investigation of another wrongdoing; s.23(2), considered in the context of s.7(7) above, grants a certain exception from liability for the person so authorised.

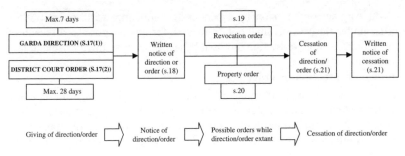

Diagram 1. Pt.3 of the Act

Direction or order not to carry out service or transaction

17.—(1) A member of the Garda Síochána not below the rank of superintendent may, by notice in writing, direct a person not to carry out any specified service or transaction during the period specified in the direction, not exceeding 7 days, if the member is satisfied that, on the basis of information that the Garda Síochána has obtained or received (whether or not in a report made under *Chapter 4* of *Part 4*), such a direction is reasonably necessary to enable the Garda Síochána to carry out preliminary investigations into whether or not there are reasonable grounds to suspect that the service or transaction would, if it were to proceed, comprise or assist in money laundering or terrorist financing.

(2) A judge of the District Court may order a person not to carry out any specified service or transaction during the period specified in the order, not exceeding 28 days, if satisfied by information on oath of a member of the Garda Síochána, that—

(*a*) there are reasonable grounds to suspect that the service or transaction would, if it were to proceed, comprise or assist in money laundering or terrorist financing, and

(*b*) an investigation of a person for that money laundering or terrorist financing is taking place.

(3) An order may be made, under *subsection (2)*, in relation to a particular service or transaction, on more than one occasion.

(4) An application for an order under *subsection (2)* shall be made to a judge of the District Court assigned to the district in which the order is proposed to be served.

(5) A person who fails to comply with a direction or order under this section commits an offence and is liable—

(*a*) on summary conviction, to a fine not exceeding €5,000 or imprisonment for a term not exceeding 12 months (or both), or

(*b*) on conviction on indictment, to a fine or imprisonment for a term not exceeding 5 years (or both).

(6) Any act or omission by a person in compliance with a direction or order under this section shall not be treated, for any purpose, as a breach of any requirement or restriction imposed by any other enactment or rule of law.

Notice of direction or order

18.—(1) As soon as practicable after a direction is given or order is made under *section 17*, the member of the Garda Síochána who gave the direction or applied for the order shall ensure that any person who the member is aware is affected by the direction or order is given notice, in writing, of the direction or order unless—

> (*a*) it is not reasonably practicable to ascertain the whereabouts of the person, or
> (*b*) there are reasonable grounds for believing that disclosure to the person would prejudice the investigation in respect of which the direction or order is given.

(2) Notwithstanding *subsection (1)(b)*, a member of the Garda Síochána shall give notice, in writing, of a direction or order under this section to any person who is, or appears to be, affected by it as soon as practicable after the Garda Síochána becomes aware that the person is aware that the direction has been given or order has been made.

(3) Nothing in *subsection (1)* or *(2)* requires notice to be given to a person to whom a direction is given or order is addressed under this section.

(4) A notice given under this section shall include the reasons for the direction or order concerned and advise the person to whom the notice is given of the person's right to make an application under *section 19* or *20*.

(5) The reasons given in the notice need not include details the disclosure of which there are reasonable grounds for believing would prejudice the investigation in respect of which the direction is given or order is made.

Revocation of direction or order on application

19.—(1) At any time while a direction or order is in force under *section 17*, a judge of the District Court may revoke the direction or order if the judge is satisfied, on the application of a person affected by the direction or order, as the case may be, that the matters referred to in *section 17(1)* or *(2)* do not, or no longer, apply.(2) Such an application may be made only if notice has been given to the Garda Síochána in accordance with any applicable rules of court.

Order in relation to property subject of direction or order

20.—(1) At any time while a direction or order is in force under *section 17*, in relation to property, a judge of the District Court may, on application by any person affected by the direction or order concerned, as the case may be, make any order that the judge considers appropriate in relation to any of the property concerned if satisfied that it is necessary to do so for the purpose of enabling the person—

(a) to discharge the reasonable living and other necessary expenses, including legal expenses in or in relation to legal proceedings, incurred or to be incurred in respect of the person or the person's dependants, or

(b) to carry on a business, trade, profession or other occupation to which any of the property relates.

(2) Such an application may be made only if notice has been given to the Garda Síochána in accordance with any applicable rules of court.

Cessation of direction or order on cessation of investigation

21.—(1) A direction or order under *section 17* ceases to have effect on the cessation of an investigation into whether the service or transaction the subject of the direction or order would, if it were to proceed, comprise or assist in money laundering or terrorist financing.

(2) As soon as practicable after a direction or order under *section 17* ceases, as a result of *subsection (1)*, to have effect, a member of the Garda Síochána shall give notice in writing of the fact that the direction or order has ceased to have effect to—

(a) the person to whom the direction or order has been given, and

(b) any other person who the member is aware is affected by the direction or order.

Section Note

This provision, insofar as it relates to the automatic cessation of a direction made under s.17, would appear to address the difficulty that arose in *Burns v The Governor and Company of the Bank of Ireland and Others* [2007] IEHC 318 (unreported) in which the failure of the Garda authorities to lift a direction made under s.31(8) of the Criminal Justice Act 1994 at a time when they knew there was not going to be any prosecution in respect of certain funds was held by the High Court (Gilligan J.) to be *ultra vires* the powers conferred on the Garda Síochána by that (now repealed) section.

Suspicious transaction report not to be disclosed

22.—A report made under *Chapter 4* of *Part 4* shall not be disclosed, in the course of proceedings under *section 17* or *19*, to any person other than the judge of the District Court concerned.

Authorisation to proceed with act that would otherwise comprise money laundering

23.—(1) A member of the Garda Síochána not below the rank of superintendent may, by notice in writing, authorise a person to do a thing referred to in *section 7(1)* if the member is satisfied that the thing is necessary for the purposes of an investigation into an offence.

(2) The doing of any thing in accordance with an authorisation under this section shall not be treated, for any purpose, as a breach of any requirement or restriction imposed by any other enactment or rule of law.

(3) *Subsection (2)* is without prejudice to *section 7(7)*.

PART 4

Provisions Relating to Finance Services Industry, Professional Service Providers and Others

General Note

Pt.4 of the Act is the principal part of the Act. It comprises some eighty-six sections divided into ten chapters. It imposes identification, monitoring and reporting requirements on financial industry operators, professional services providers and others: these persons are in effect pressed into service in combating money laundering and terrorist financing. In general terms, Pt.4 can perhaps be viewed as realising, *inter alia*, the twenty-third of the FATF 40 Recommendations which recommends, amongst other matters, that "Countries should ensure that financial institutions are subject to adequate regulation and supervision and are effectively implementing the FATF Recommendations" (see FATF, *FATF 40 Recommendations*, p. 9). Ch.1 of Pt.4 (ss.24 to 30) defines various terms used in Pt.4. Ch.2 (ss.31 and 32) is concerned with the designation of places having requirements equivalent to the Directive and places having inadequate procedures for the detection of money laundering or terrorist financing. Chapters 3 to 6 are of particular relevance to all designated persons. Ch.3 (ss.33 to 40) is concerned with customer due diligence (or "CDD"). Ch.4 (ss.41 to 47) is concerned with the reporting of suspicious transactions and of transactions involving certain places. Ch.5 (ss.48 to 53) is concerned with tipping off by designated persons. Ch.6 (ss.54 and 55) is concerned with the internal policies, procedures, training and record-keeping of and/or by designated persons. Ch.7 (ss.56 to 59) makes certain special provision as regards credit and financial institutions. Ch.8 (ss.60 to 83) is concerned with the monitoring of designated persons by regulators and other competent authorities. Ch.9 (ss.84 to 106) is concerned with the authorisation of trust or company service providers. Ch.10 (ss.107 to 109), amongst other matters, provides for the approval of guidelines by the Minister and makes provision in respect of certain persons, who are effectively directing particular private members' clubs at which gambling activities are carried on.

CHAPTER 1

Interpretation (Part 4)

Definitions

24.—(1) In this Part—

"barrister" means a practising barrister;

"beneficial owner" has the meaning assigned to it by *sections 26* to *30*;

"business relationship", in relation to a designated person and a customer of the person, means a business, professional or commercial relationship between the person and the customer that the person expects to be ongoing;

"competent authority" has the meaning assigned to it by *sections 60* and *61*;

"credit institution" means—

(a) a credit institution within the meaning of Article 4(1) of the Recast Banking Consolidation Directive, or

(b) An Post in respect of any activity that it carries out, whether as principal or agent, that would render it, or a principal for whom it is an agent, a credit institution as a result of the application of *paragraph (a)*;

"customer"—

(a) in relation to an auditor, means—

(i) a body corporate to which the auditor has been appointed as an auditor, or

(ii) in the case of an auditor appointed to audit the accounts of an unincorporated body of persons or of an individual, the unincorporated body or the individual,

(b) in relation to a relevant independent legal professional, includes, in the case of the provision of services by a barrister, a person who is a client of a solicitor seeking advice from the barrister for or on behalf of the client and does not, in that case, include the solicitor, or

(c) in relation to a trust or company service provider, means a person with whom the trust or company service provider has an arrangement to provide services as such a service provider;

"Department" means the Department of Justice, Equality and Law Reform;

"designated accountancy body" means a prescribed accountancy body, within the meaning of Part 2 of the Companies (Auditing and Accounting) Act 2003;

"designated person" has the meaning assigned to it by *section 25*;

"EEA State" means a state that is a Contracting Party to the Agreement on the European Economic Area signed at Oporto on 2 May 1992, as adjusted by the Protocol signed at Brussels on 17 March 1993;

"Electronic Money Directive" means Directive 2009/110/EC of the European Parliament and of the Council of 16 September 2009 on the taking up, pursuit and prudential supervision of the business of electronic money institutions amending Directives 2005/60/EC and 2006/48/EC and repealing Directive 2000/46/EC;[5]

"external accountant" means a person who by way of business provides accountancy services (other than when providing such services to the

---

[5] OJ L267, 10.10.2009, p.7.

employer of the person) whether or not the person holds accountancy qualifications or is a member of a designated accountancy body;
"financial institution" means—

(a) an undertaking that carries out one or more of the activities listed in points 2 to 12, 14 and 15 of Annex I to the Recast Banking Consolidation Directive (the text of which is set out for convenience of reference in *Schedule2*) or foreign exchange services, but does not include an undertaking—
  (i) that does not carry out any of the activities listed in those points other than one or more of the activities listed in point 7, and
  (ii) whose only customers (if any) are members of the same group as the undertaking,

(b) an insurance company that carries out the activities covered by the Life Assurance Consolidation Directive and is authorised in accordance with that Directive,

(c) a person, other than a person falling within Article 2 of the Markets in Financial Instruments Directive, whose regular occupation or business is—
  (i) the provision to other persons of an investment service, within the meaning of that Directive, or
  (ii) the performance of an investment activity within the meaning of that Directive,

(d) an investment business firm within the meaning of the Investment Intermediaries Act 1995 (other than a nonlife insurance intermediary within the meaning of that Act),

(e) a collective investment undertaking that markets or otherwise offers its units or shares,

(f) an insurance intermediary within the meaning of the Insurance Mediation Directive (other than a tied insurance intermediary within the meaning of that Directive) that provides life assurance or other investment related services, or

(g) An Post, in respect of any activity it carries out, whether as principal or agent—
  (i) that would render it, or a principal for whom it is an agent, a financial institution as a result of the application of any of the foregoing paragraphs,
  (ii) that is listed in point 1 of Annex I to the Recast Banking Consolidation Directive, or
  (iii) that would render it, or a principal for whom it is an agent, an investment business firm within the meaning of the Investment Intermediaries Act 1995 (other than a non-life insurance intermediary within the meaning of that Act) if section 2(6) of that Act did not apply;

"group", other than in the definition in this subsection of "public body", has the same meaning as in Directive 2002/87/EC of the European Parliament and of the Council of 16 December 2002 on the supplementary supervision of credit institutions, insurance undertakings and investment firms in a financial conglomerate and amending Council Directives 73/239/EEC, 79/267/EEC, 92/49/EEC, 92/96/EEC, 93/6/EEC and 93/22/EEC, and Directives 98/78/EC and 2000/12/EC of the European Parliament and of the Council;[6]

"Insurance Mediation Directive" means Directive 2002/92/EC of the European Parliament and of the Council of 9 December 2002 on insurance mediation;[7]

"Life Assurance Consolidation Directive" means Directive 2002/83/EC of the European Parliament and of the Council of November 2002 concerning life assurance;[8]

"Markets in Financial Instruments Directive" means Directive 2004/39/EC of the European Parliament and of the Council of 21 April 2004 on markets in financial instruments amending Council Directives 85/611/EEC and 93/6/EEC and Directive 2000/12/EC of the European Parliament and of the Council and repealing Council Directive 93/22/EEC;[9]

"member", in relation to a designated accountancy body, means a member, within the meaning of Part 2 of the Companies (Auditing and Accounting) Act 2003, of a designated accountancy body;

"member", in relation to the Irish Taxation Institute, means a person who is subject to the professional and ethical standards of the Institute, including its investigation and disciplinary procedures, but does not include a person who is admitted to its membership as a student;

"occasional transaction", in relation to a customer of a designated person, means a single transaction, or a series of transactions that are or appear to be linked to each other, where—

(a) the designated person does not have a business relationship with the customer, and

(b) the total amount of money paid by the customer in the single transaction or series is greater than €15,000;

"payment service" has the same meaning as in the Payment Services Directive;

"Payment Services Directive" means Directive 2007/64/EC of the European Parliament and of the Council of 13 November 2007 on payment services in the internal market amending Directives 97/7/EC, 2002/65/EC, 2005/60/EC and 2006/48/EC and repealing Directive 97/5/EC;[10]

---

[6] OJ L35, 11.2.2003, p.1.
[7] OJ L9, 15.1.2003, p.3.
[8] OJ L345, 19.12.2002, p.1.
[9] OJ L145, 30.4.2004, p.1.
[10] OJ L319, 5.12.2007, p.1.

"professional service provider" means an auditor, external accountant, tax adviser, relevant independent legal professional or trust or company service provider;

"property service provider" means a person who by way of business carries out any of the following services in respect of property located in or outside the State:

(*a*) the auction of property other than land;

(*b*) the purchase or sale, by whatever means, of land;

but does not include a service provided by a local authority in the course of the performance of its statutory functions under any statutory provision;

"public body" means a body, organisation or group—

(*a*) specified in paragraph 1(1) to (4) of the First Schedule to the Freedom of Information Act 1997 (including as construed by paragraph 4 of that Schedule), or

(*b*) established by or under an enactment and prescribed by regulations for the purposes of paragraph 1(5) of the First Schedule to that Act;

"Recast Banking Consolidation Directive" means Directive 2006/48/EC of the European Parliament and of the Council of 14 June 2006 relating to the taking up and pursuit of the business of credit institutions (recast)[11], as amended by the following:

(*a*) the Payment Services Directive;

(*b*) the Electronic Money Directive;

"regulated market" means—

(*a*) a regulated financial market that is in an EEA State and is included in any list published by the European Commission (including any list on the Commission's website), and in force, under Article 47 of the Markets in Financial Instruments Directive,

(*b*) a regulated financial market in a place other than an EEA State, being a place that imposes, on companies whose securities are admitted to trading on the market, disclosure requirements consistent with legislation of the European Communities, or

(*c*) a prescribed regulated financial market;

"relevant independent legal professional" means a barrister, solicitor or notary who carries out any of the following services:

(*a*) the provision of assistance in the planning or execution of transactions for clients concerning any of the following:

---

[11] OJ L177, 30.6.2006, p.1.

(i) buying or selling land or business entities;

(ii) managing the money, securities or other assets of clients;

(iii) opening or managing bank, savings or securities accounts;

(iv) organising contributions necessary for the creation, operation or management of companies;

(v) creating, operating or managing trusts, companies or similar structures or arrangements;

(b) acting for or on behalf of clients in financial transactions or transactions relating to land;

"relevant professional adviser" means an accountant, auditor or tax adviser who is a member of a designated accountancy body or of the Irish Taxation Institute;

"solicitor" means a practising solicitor;

"State competent authority" has the meaning assigned to it by *section 62*;

"tax adviser" means a person who by way of business provides advice about the tax affairs of other persons;

"transaction" means—

(a) in relation to a professional service provider, any transaction that is carried out in connection with a customer of the provider and that is—

(i) in the case of a provider acting as an auditor, the subject of an audit carried out by the provider in respect of the accounts of the customer,

(ii) in the case of a provider acting as an external accountant or tax adviser, or as a trust or company service provider, the subject of a service carried out by the provider for the customer, or

(iii) in the case of a provider acting as a relevant independent legal professional, the subject of a service carried out by the professional for the customer of a kind referred to in *paragraph (a) or (b)* of the definition of "relevant independent legal professional" in this subsection;

and

(b) in relation to a casino or private members' club, a transaction, such as the purchase or exchange of tokens or chips, or the placing of a bet, carried out in connection with gambling activities carried out on the premises of the casino or club by a customer of the casino or club;

"trust or company service provider" means any person whose business it is to provide any of the following services:

(a) forming companies or other bodies corporate;

(b) acting as a director or secretary of a company under an arrangement with a person other than the company;

(c) arranging for another person to act as a director or secretary of a company;

(d) acting, or arranging for a person to act, as a partner of a partnership;

(e) providing a registered office, business address, correspondence or administrative address or other related services for a body corporate or partnership;

(f) acting, or arranging for another person to act, as a trustee of a trust;

(g) acting, or arranging for another person to act, as a nominee shareholder for a person other than a company whose securities are listed on a regulated market.

(2) The Minister may prescribe a regulated financial market for the purposes of the definition of "regulated market" in *subsection (1)* only if the Minister is satisfied that the market is in a place other than an EEA State that imposes, on companies whose securities are admitted to trading on the market, disclosure requirements consistent with legislation of the European Communities.

Section Note

"beneficial owner"

The term beneficial owner is defined over five provisions (ss.26 to 30) of the Act. A summary table outlining the effect of those provisions is set out in the consideration of s.26 below.

"business relationship"

A designated person must expect a business, professional or commercial relationship to be ongoing before it may constitute a "business relationship" for the purposes of the Act. A good example of a business transaction that would likely not constitute a "business relationship" would be the foreign exchange services provided by high street credit institutions. Typically such foreign exchange services are made available to both accountholders and non-accountholders with the relevant credit institution. In performing a foreign exchange transaction for a non-accountholder who avails of a credit institution's foreign exchange on a one-off or perhaps even irregular basis, it is unlikely that a credit institution expects the relationship between it and that non-accountholder to be ongoing and thus the relationship does not constitute a "business relationship". It does not matter that a customer may expect a relationship between it and a designated person to be ongoing; it is only the expectation of the designated person that is relevant.

"credit institution"

The definition of what constitutes a "credit institution" is relatively complex. Insofar as a ready reading of the Act is concerned, it is perhaps to be regretted that the definition cross-refers into EU legislation as it does. At the time of writing, the term "credit institution" is defined in Art.4(1) of the Recast Banking Consolidation Directive, as amended, to mean "an undertaking the business of which is to receive deposits or other repayable funds from the public and to grant credits for its own account". (Directive 2006/48 relating to the taking up and pursuit of the business of credit institutions (recast) (O.J. L177,

30.6.2006, p.1), as amended by Directives 2007/64/EC and Directive 2009/110/EC (see especially Art.20 of the latter)). Thus, at the time of writing, a credit institution for the purposes of s.24(1) of the Act means a credit institution as defined aforesaid or An Post in respect of the activities described.

"customer"

Given the centrality of the term "customer" to much of Ch.3 it is perhaps to be regretted that the Act did not give a more comprehensive definition of this term than the rather limited definition in s.24(1). It is clear from the definition of "business relationship" that a customer relationship may arise relatively quickly for the purposes of the Act between a supplier and a customer. This is because a "business relationship" (which itself arises when a designated person expects a business, professional or commercial relationship with a customer to be ongoing) is predicated on there already being a customer relationship in place. As such an expectation can be formed relatively quickly, this suggests that a customer relationship can be formed even more quickly. It would seem prudent to assume that a person becomes a customer at the moment that such person places custom with a supplier and it is at least conceivable that a customer relationship could be found to arise where a person approaches a supplier with a view to placing custom with that supplier.

"designated accountancy body"

At the time of writing, the following bodies are prescribed accountancy bodies within the meaning of Pt.2 of the Companies (Auditing and Accounting) Act 2003 (per s.4(1) of that Act): any body of accountants recognised for the purposes of s.187 of the Companies Act 1990; and any other body of accountants that is prescribed under s.48(1)(a) of the 2003 Act. Under regulation 2 of the Companies (Auditing and Accounting) Act 2003 (Prescribed Accountancy Bodies) Regulations 2006 (S.I. No. 57 of 2006) the following bodies of accountants are prescribed for the purposes of s.48(1)(a) of the 2003 Act: The Association of International Accountants; The Chartered Institute of Management Accountants; and The Chartered Institute of Public Finance and Accountancy.

"Department"

Since the enactment of the Act, the Department of Justice, Equality and Law Reform has been re-named the Department of Justice and Law Reform by the Justice, Equality and Law Reform (Alteration of Name of Department and Title of Minister) Order 2010 (S.I. No. 216 of 2010).

"EEA State"

At the time of writing this definition extends to the 27 EU Member States plus Iceland, Liechtenstein and Norway.

"financial institution"
There are seven main categories of financial institution within this
definition. All of them cross-refer into other legislation.

(a) *Certain entities engaged in banking activities*
 The relevant text of the Recast Banking Consolidation Directive
 is set out in Schedule 2 of the Act.

(b) *Certain insurance companies*
 The "Life Assurance Consolidation Directive" (itself a defined
 term in s.24(1)) is concerned with the taking-up and pursuit of
 the self-employed activity of direct insurance by undertakings
 that are established in an EU Member State or wish to become
 established there doing the activities mentioned hereafter: first,
 the following kinds of assurance where they are on a contractual
 basis, namely life assurance, annuities, supplementary insurance and permanent health insurance not subject to cancella-
 tion; second, operations such as those listed hereafter, where
 they are on a contractual basis, and insofar as subject to
 supervision by the administrative authorities responsible for the
 supervision of private insurance, namely tontines, certain capital
 redemption operations, management of group pension funds,
 and certain assurance activities under French law. (Life
 Assurance Consolidation Directive, Art.2).

(c) *Certain persons not falling within Art.2 of the MiFID Directive*
 The particular difficulty posed by this definition is that there
 is such an array of persons "falling within" (by which the Act
 presumably means "referred to in") Article 2 of the MiFID
 Directive, *viz.* (a) insurance undertakings; (b) persons that
 provide investment services exclusively for their parent undertakings, for their subsidiaries or for other subsidiaries of their
 parent undertakings; (c) persons providing an investment
 service where that service is provided in an incidental manner
 in the course of a professional activity and that activity is
 regulated by legal or regulatory provisions or a code of ethics
 governing the profession which do not exclude the provision of
 that service; (d) persons who do not provide any investment
 services or activities other than dealing on own account unless
 they are market makers or deal on own account outside a
 regulated market or a multilateral trading facility on an organised,
 frequent and systematic basis by providing a system accessible to
 third parties in order to engage in dealings with them; (e) persons
 which provide investment services consisting exclusively in the
 administration of employee-participation schemes; (f) persons
 which provide investment services which only involve both
 administration of employee-participation schemes and the
 provision of investment services exclusively for their parent
 undertakings, for their subsidiaries or for other subsidiaries of
 their parent undertakings; (g) the members of the European
 System of Central Banks and other national bodies performing
 similar functions and other public bodies charged with or

intervening in the management of the public debt; (h) collective investment undertakings and pensions funds whether coordinated at Community level or not and the depositaries and managers of such undertakings; (i) persons dealing on own account in financial instruments or providing investment services in specified commodity derivatives or derivative contracts to the clients of their main business, provided this is an ancillary activity to their main business, when considered on a group basis, and that business is not the provision of investment services within the MiFID Directive or banking services under Directive 2000/12/EC of the European Parliament and of the Council of 20 May 2000 relating to the taking up and pursuit of the business of credit institution (O.J. L126, 26.5.2000, p.1); (j) persons providing investment advice in the course of providing another professional activity not covered by the MiFID Directive provided that the provision of such advice is not specifically remunerated; (k) in certain instances, persons whose main business consists of dealing on own account in commodities and/or commodity derivatives; (l) firms which provide investment services and/or perform investment activities consisting exclusively in dealing on own account on markets in financial futures or options or other derivatives and on cash markets for the sole purpose of hedging positions on derivatives markets or which deal for the accounts of other members of those markets or make prices for them and which are guaranteed by clearing members of the same markets, where responsibility for ensuring the performance of contracts entered into by such firms is assumed by clearing members of the same markets; (m) certain Danish, Finnish and Italian entities.

Having determined that a person does not fall within any of the above categories, the next question to be resolved in order that one can determine whether such a person is a "financial institution" for the purposes of Pt.4 is whether that person's regular occupation or business is the provision to others of an "investment service" or the performance of an "investment activity", in each case within the meaning of the MiFID Directive. The term "investment services and activities" is defined in Art.4(1) of the MiFID Directive as meaning any of the services and activities listed in Section A of Annex I of that Directive and relating to any of the instruments listed in Section C of Annex I of that Directive. Section A of Annex I refers to the following investment services and activities: (1) reception and transmission of orders in relation to one or more financial instruments; (2) execution of orders on behalf of clients; (3) dealing on own account; (4) portfolio management; (5) investment advice; (6) underwriting of financial instruments and/or placing of financial instruments on a firm commitment basis; (7) placing of financial instruments without a firm commitment basis; and (8) operation of multilateral trading facilities. The financial instruments listed in Section C of Annex I are: (1) transferable securities; (2) money-market instruments; (3) units in collective investment undertakings; (4) options, futures, swaps, forward rate agreements and any other derivative contracts relating to securities, currencies, interest rates or yields, or other derivatives instruments, financial indices or financial measures which may be settled physically or in cash; (5) options, futures, swaps, forward rate agreements and any other derivative contracts relating to commodities that must be settled in cash or may be settled in cash at the option of one of the parties (otherwise than by reason of a default or other termination event); (6) options, futures, swaps, and any other derivative contract relating to commodities that can be physically settled provided that they are traded on a regulated market and/or a multilateral trading facility; (7) options, futures, swaps and any other derivative contracts relating to commodities, that can be physically settled not otherwise mentioned in (6) and not being for commercial purposes, which have the characteristics of other derivative financial instruments, having regard to whether, *inter alia*, they are cleared and settled through recognised clearing houses or are subject to regular margin calls; (8) derivative instruments for the transfer of credit risk; (9) financial contracts for differences; (10) options, futures, swaps, forward rate agreements and any other derivative contracts relating to climatic variables, freight rates, emission allowances or inflation rates or other official economic statistics that must be settled in cash or may be settled in cash at the option of one of the parties (otherwise than by reason of a default or other termination event), as well as any other derivative contracts relating to assets, rights, obligations, indices and measures not otherwise mentioned in Section C, which have the characteristics of other derivative financial instruments, having regard to whether, *inter alia*, they are traded on a regulated market or a multilateral trading facility, are cleared and settled through recognised clearing houses or are subject to regular margin calls.

(d) *Certain investment business firms within the meaning of the Investment Intermediaries Act 1995.*

An investment business firm for the purposes of the 1995 Act (per s.2(1) of that Act) is any person other than a stock exchange member who provides one or more investment business services or investment advice to a third party on a professional basis, the 1995 Act providing an exhaustive definition of what constitute "investment business services" and "investment advice", both of which terms also involve reference to the (again exhaustively defined term) "investment instruments".

(e) *Certain collective investment undertakings*

(f) *Certain insurance intermediaries*

An insurance intermediary within the meaning of the "Insurance Mediation Directive" (itself a defined term) is, per Art.2(5) of same, "any natural or legal person who for remuneration, takes up or pursues insurance mediation". The term "insurance mediation" is defined in Art.2(3) of the Insurance Mediation Directive as meaning "the activities of introducing, proposing or carrying out other work preparatory to the conclusion of contracts of insurance, or of concluding such contracts, or of assisting in the administration and performance of such contracts, in particular in the event of a claim. These activities when undertaken by an insurance undertaking or an employee of an insurance undertaking who is acting under the responsibility of the insurance undertaking shall not be considered as insurance mediation. The provision of information on an incidental basis in the context of another professional activity provided that the purpose of that activity is not to assist the customer in concluding or performing an insurance contract, the management of claims of an insurance undertaking on a professional basis, and loss adjusting and expert appraisal of claims shall also not be considered as insurance mediation". The term "financial institution" only applies to such insurance intermediaries as provide life assurance or other investment-related activities and which are not tied insurance intermediaries. A "tied insurance intermediary" within the meaning of the Insurance Mediation Directive is "any person who carries on the activity of insurance mediation for and on behalf of one or more insurance undertakings in the case of insurance products which are not in competition, but does not collect premiums or amounts intended for the customer and who acts under the full responsibility of those insurance undertakings for the products which concern them respectively" (Insurance Mediation Directive, Art.2(7)).

(g) *An Post in certain circumstances*

An Post only constitutes a "financial institution" in the circumstances defined in s.24(1). The current text of Annex I to the Recast Banking Consolidation Directive is set out in Schedule 2 of the Act.

"group"

Article 2(12) of Directive 2002/87/EC defines the term "group" to mean a group of undertakings which consists of a parent undertaking, its subsidiaries and the entities in which the parent undertaking or its subsidiaries hold a "participation" (as defined in Art.2(11) of that Directive), as well as undertakings linked to each other by a relationship within the meaning of Seventh Council Directive 83/349/EEC of 13 June 1983 based on the Art.54(3)(g) of the Treaty on consolidated accounts (O.J. L193, 18.07.1983, p.1).

"*member*"

The term "member" as defined in Pt.2 of the Companies (Auditing and Accounting) Act 2003 means, in relation to a prescribed accountancy body, (a) a person or (b) a firm that is, or was at the relevant time, subject to the investigation and disciplinary procedures approved under s.9(2)(c) of the 2003 Act for that body.

"*payment service*"

The term "payment service" when used in the "Payment Services Directive" (itself a defined term in s.24(1)) means any business activity listed in the Annex to the Directive. The listed business activities are: (1) services enabling cash to be placed on a "payment account" as well as all the operations required for operating a payment account; (2) services enabling cash withdrawals from a payment account as well as all the operations required for operating a payment account; (3) execution of "payment transactions", including transfers of funds on a payment account with the user's payment service provider or with another payment service provider; (4) execution of payment transactions where the funds are covered by a credit line for a payment service user; (5) issuing and/or acquiring "payment instruments"; (6) money remittance; and (7) execution of payment transactions where the consent of the payer to execute a payment transaction is given by means of any telecommunication, digital or IT device and the payment is made to the telecommunication, IT system or network operator, acting only as an intermediary between the payment service user and the supplier of the goods and services. The quoted terms are also defined in the Payment Services Directive. Thus: a "payment account" (per Art.4(14) of the Payment Services Directive) is an account held in the name of one or more payment service users which is used for the execution of payment transactions; a "payment transaction" (per Art. 4(5)), is an act, initiated by the payer/payee, of placing, transferring or withdrawing funds, irrespective of any underlying obligations between the payer and payee; and a "payment instrument" (per Art.4(23)) is any personalised device/s and/or set of procedures agreed between the payment service user and the payment service provider and used by the payment service user in order to initiate a payment order.

"*professional service provider*"

There are a number of defined terms within this definition, namely "external accountant", "tax adviser", "relevant independent legal professional" and "trust or company service provider". During the legislative process which preceded the enactment of the Act it was proposed that the definition should be expanded to refer also to an "insolvency practitioner". Thus, for example, during the Report and Final Stages of the Seanad debates on the Bill, Senator Ivana Bacik stated:

> "I am concerned that the existing provisions of the Bill do not cover those persons who hold themselves out as "insolvency

> practitioners", that is, persons who act as liquidators, provisional liquidators, receivers, examiners, trustees in bankruptcy proceedings or administrators under the insurance and credit union Acts. Such persons will be captured if they are members of a designated accountancy body or the Irish Taxation Institute in accordance with the Minister's amendments. However, he has acknowledged that these persons may not hold accountancy qualifications and may not be members of a designated accountancy body, the Irish Taxation Institute or a legal professional body. In the interests of ensuring adequate consumer protection, it is important, therefore, to include a term that would capture a group which may not otherwise be captured. The Minister described them as "amateur practitioners", but a consumer dealing with someone who holds himself or herself out as an insolvency practitioner may not be aware of the professional or amateur status of the person concerned. Chartered Accountants Ireland has also suggested it would be useful to include the term "insolvency practitioner" in the Bill." (202(2) *Díospóireachtaí Parlaiminte* (Seanad Éireann) (21.4.10), p.74, *et seq*).

Senator Bacik's proposed amendment was not accepted by the Minister for Justice, Equality and Law Reform, effectively on the basis that it went further than the Directive required. The Minister acknowledged that it was of course possible to go further than the Directive required (pursuant to Art.5 of the Directive, though only to adopt or retain in force stricter provisions in the field covered by the Directive). However, the Minister indicated that a further group should not be included in the definition of "professional service provider" without more detailed consideration and analysis of matters and that it would be possible to make such an extension in the future by way of secondary legislation. (202(2) *Díospóireachtaí Parlaiminte* (Seanad Éireann) (21.4.10), p.75).

"property service provider"
This definition attracted some attention during the Second Stage reading by the Seanad of the Bill with Senator Ivana Bacik suggesting that:

> "Many ordinary individuals under the Celtic tiger years could easily now be described as property service providers. Will all of the onerous obligations under section 55 which deals with record keeping and section 54 which deals with internal policies, procedures and training apply to them?". (201(4) *Díospóireachtaí Parlaiminte* (Seanad Éireann) (2.3.10), p.220).

Provided such individuals are "by way of business" carrying out any of the services referred to in the definition of "property service provider" in respect of property in or outside Ireland, they would constitute property service providers and hence, by virtue of s.25(1)(f) of the Act, would be designated persons and so subject to s.55 of the Act.

However, it is perhaps open to question just how many ordinary individuals would in practice be providing one or more of the services referred to in the definition and doing so "by way of business". Perhaps a greater risk arising for such individuals is where, for example, an individual has established a company that buys and/or sells land and has been an officer/manager of that company. If that company was found to provide the service to its owners of buying or selling land "by way of business", then that company would be a property service provider and its officers/managers could, by virtue of s.111 of the Act, be exposed to criminal liability for any failure by that company to comply with certain provisions of the Act.

"public body"
At the time of writing a wide array of Government departments and public bodies come within this definition.

"regulated market"
Art.47 of the MiFID Directive requires of each EU Member State that it draw up a list of the regulated markets for which it is the home Member State and forward that list to the other Member States and the European Commission. Certain constraints on the financial markets that can be prescribed by the Minister in this regard are established in s.24(2) of the Act. The Irish Stock Exchange is a regulated market but its IEX market is not.

"relevant independent legal professional"
It seems unlikely that there are many solicitors in private practice who are not carrying out one or more of the services referred to in this definition. By contrast, it is eminently conceivable that there are many practising barristers who are not providing any of these services, such is the nature of their work. The term "notary" is not defined in the Act but would appear, at least, to embrace notaries public. (A notary public is a public officer constituted by law to serve the public in non-contentious matters usually concerned with foreign or international business through, *inter alia*, administering oaths, attesting signatures, authenticating documents, giving notarial acts, taking affidavits (other than for the courts in Ireland), taking affirmations and declarations, receiving and making protests under mercantile law, issuing notarial certificates in respect of documents and persons and drawing up powers of attorney and other legal documents customarily prepared by notaries public). That said, the term "notaries" is employed in the relevant provision of the Directive (Art.2(3)) and thus, by virtue of s.2(2) of the Act the near-identical reference to a "notary" in the Act must be construed to bear the meaning given that term in the Directive, absent contrary intention (and there is no such contrary intention expressed in the Act). The list of services referred to in the definition is broader than the relevant list contained in the twelfth of the FATF 40 Recommendations (see FATF, *FATF 40 Recommendations*, p.7). For a recent account of the role of the notary public under

Irish law see Hall, E., "The Right Note" (2010) 104(9) *Law Society Gazette* 40.

"relevant professional adviser"
Any accountant is a "relevant professional adviser". This makes the definition of who constitutes a "relevant professional adviser" wider in this regard than is anticipated in the twelfth of the FATF 40 Recommendations. (See FATF, *FATF 40 Recommendations*, p.7). The definition only refers to certain tax advisers, not to every "tax adviser" within the meaning of s.24(1).

Meaning of "designated person"

25.—(1) In this Part, "designated person" means any person, acting in the State in the course of business carried on by the person in the State, who or that is—

(*a*) a credit institution, except as provided by *subsection (4)*,

(*b*) a financial institution, except as provided by *subsection (4)*,

(*c*) an auditor, external accountant or tax adviser,

(*d*) a relevant independent legal professional,

(*e*) a trust or company service provider,

(*f*) a property service provider,

(*g*) a casino,

(*h*) a person who effectively directs a private members' club at which gambling activities are carried on, but only in respect of those gambling activities,

(*i*) any person trading in goods, but only in respect of transactions involving payments, to the person in cash, of a total of at least €15,000 (whether in one transaction or in a series of transactions that are or appear to be linked to each other), or

(*j*) any other person of a prescribed class.

(2) For the purposes of this Part, a person is to be treated as a designated person only in respect of those activities or services that render the person a designated person.

(3) A reference in this Part to a designated person does not include a reference to any of the following:

(*a*) the Minister for Finance;

(*b*) the Central Bank and Financial Services Authority of Ireland;

(*c*) the National Treasury Management Agency.

(4) A person is not to be treated as a designated person for the purposes of this Part solely as a result of operating as a credit institution or financial institution, in the course of business, if—

(*a*) the annual turnover of the person's business that is attributable to operating as a credit institution or financial institution is €70,000 (or such other amount as may be prescribed) or less,

(b) the total of any single transaction, or a series of transactions that are or appear to be linked to each other, in respect of which the person operates as a credit institution or financial institution does not exceed €1,000 (or such other lesser amount as may be prescribed),

(c) the annual turnover of the person's business that is attributable to operating as a credit institution or financial institution does not exceed 5 per cent of the business's total annual turnover,

(d) the person's operation as a credit institution or financial institution is directly related and ancillary to the person's main business activity, and

(e) the person provides services when operating as a credit institution or financial institution only to persons who are customers in respect of the person's main business activity, rather than to members of the public in general.

(5) *Subsection (4)* does not apply in relation to any prescribed class of person.

(6) For the avoidance of doubt and without prejudice to the generality of *subsection (1)(a)* or *(b)*, a credit or financial institution that acts in the State in the course of business carried on by the institution in the State, by means of a branch situated in the State, is a designated person whether or not the institution is incorporated, or the head office of the institution is situated, in a place other than in the State.

(7) The Minister may prescribe a class of persons for the purposes of *subsection (1)(j)* only if the Minister is satisfied that any of the business activities engaged in by the class—

(a) may be used for the purposes of—
   (i)   money laundering,
   (ii) terrorist financing, or
   (iii) an offence that corresponds or is similar to money laundering or terrorist financing under the law of a place outside the State,
   or

(b) are of a kind likely to result in members of the class obtaining information on the basis of which they may become aware of, or suspect, the involvement of customers or others in money laundering or terrorist financing.

(8) The Minister may, in any regulations made under *subsection (7)* prescribing a class of persons, apply to the class such exemptions from, or modifications to, provisions of this Act as the Minister considers appropriate, having regard to any risk that the business activities engaged in by the class may be used for a purpose referred to in *paragraph (a)* of that subsection.

(9) The Minister may prescribe an amount for the purposes of *paragraph (a)* or *(b)* of *subsection (4)*, in relation to a person's business activities as a credit institution or financial institution, only if the Minister is satisfied

that, in prescribing the amount, the purposes of that subsection will likely be fulfilled, including that—

    (*a*) those activities are carried out by the person on a limited basis, and
    (*b*) there is little risk that those activities may be used for a purpose referred to in *subsection (7)(a)*.

(10) The Minister may prescribe a class of persons for the purpose of *subsection (5)* only if the Minister is satisfied that the application of *subsection (4)* to the class involves an unacceptable risk that the business activities engaged in by the class may be used for a purpose referred to in *subsection (7)(a)*.

Section Note

Section 25(1) identifies which categories of person constitute a "designated person" for the purposes of the Pt.4. The notion of "designated person" replaces that of "designated bodies" which pertained under the Criminal Justice Act 1994. Notably, among the types of business referred to in s.25(1) of the Act is that of casino (see s.25(1)(g)). The operation of a casino of a type anticipated by the Directive remains illegal in Ireland (as most casino-style games constitute unlawful gaming). However, provision is made in the Act (see s.109) as regards the registration of certain persons who effectively direct a private members' club in Ireland at which gambling activities are carried on.

Section 25(2) makes clear that a designated person is only to be treated as such in respect of those activities or services which render him such. This provision is perhaps of especial significance for designated persons who are natural persons (*e.g.* practising barristers and solicitors) and for whom it would be impossible if every aspect of their lives had to be viewed through the prism of their being a designated person.

Section 25(3), (4) and (5) between them further refine the definition of "designated person" and except certain persons from the scope of the definition, *viz.* the Minister for Finance, the Central Bank of Ireland (per s.25(3)(b) as amended by the Central Bank Reform Act 2010 (No. 23 of 2010), s.15(14) and Schedule 2, Pt.14), the NTMA and also certain persons who might otherwise come within the definition of "credit institution" or "financial institution" but where the scale or the nature of their business is, for example, so small as to merit exception.

Section 25(5) allows the Minister for Justice and Law Reform in effect to dis-apply s.25(4) in respect of any prescribed class of person but s.25(10) only allows such prescription where the Minister is satisfied that the application of the s.25(4) exception to the class of persons he prescribes would involve an "unacceptable risk" (presumably unacceptable to the Minister) that such class of persons would engage in money laundering, terrorist financing or an offence that corresponds or is similar to money laundering or terrorist financing under the law of a place outside Ireland.

Section 25(6) makes clear that a branch office in Ireland, in effect of a non-local credit institution or financial institution, is a designated person (unless s.25(4) applies). Section 25 does not make express provision as regards a credit or financial institution that is providing services to the public in Ireland from, for example, another EU Member State, and which does not have a branch presence in Ireland.

Section 25(7), as supplemented by s.25(8), provides which additional classes of persons the Minister for Justice and Law Reform may prescribe as designated persons and on what basis. At the time of writing, no additional classes of person have been prescribed by the Minister.

Section 25(9) qualifies the extent to which the exceptions at s.25(4)(a) and (b) may be varied by way of ministerial prescription.

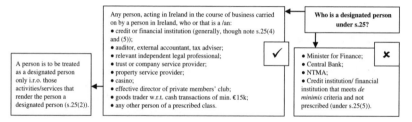

Diagram 2. Who is a "designated person"?

Beneficial owner in relation to bodies corporate

26.—In this Part, "beneficial owner", in relation to a body corporate, means any individual who—

(a) in the case of a body corporate other than a company having securities listed on a regulated market, ultimately owns or controls, whether through direct or indirect ownership or control (including through bearer shareholdings), more than 25 per cent of the shares or voting rights in the body, or

(b) otherwise exercises control over the management of the body.

Section Note

Recital 9 to the Directive states, *inter alia*, that "it is appropriate, in accordance with the new international standards, to introduce more specific and detailed provisions relating to the identification of the customer and of any beneficial owner and the verification of their identity. To that end a precise definition of 'beneficial owner' is essential". In the Directive this definition appears in Art.3(6). In the Act, ss.26 to 30 identify in detail who constitutes a beneficial owner for the purposes of Pt.4. These provisions are summarised in Table 1 below. As a rule of thumb, the "rule of 25" is often a good guide to identifying a beneficial owner. Thus the beneficial owner of: (1) a body corporate, includes any individual who, in the case of a body corporate not having securities listed on a regulated market, directly or indirectly owns or controls more than 25% of the body's shares/voting rights; (2) a partnership, includes any individual who directly or indirectly is entitled to or controls a greater than 25% share of the capital, greater than 25% share of the profits, or greater than 25% of voting rights; (3) a trust that administers and distributes funds, includes any individual entitled to a vested interest in possession, remainder or reversion in at least 25% of the capital of the trust property; (4) any other arrangement or entity that administers and distributes funds, includes any individual who benefits from at least 25% of the property of the arrangement or entity (if the individuals who benefit have been determined and also any individual who exercises control over at least 25% of the property of the entity or arrangement.

Table 1: Who is a "beneficial owner"?

BODY CORPORATE	• Any individual who (a) in the case of a body corporate not having securities listed on a regulated market, directly or indirectly owns or controls >25% of the body's shares/ voting rights or (b) otherwise exercises control over body's management. (s.26).
PARTNERSHIP	• Any individual who (a) directly or indirectly is entitled to or controls >25% share of capital, >25% share of profits, or > 25% of voting rights, or (b) otherwise exercises control over the partnership management. (s.27).
TRUST THAT ADMINISTERS AND DISTRIBUTES FUNDS	• Any individual entitled to a vested interest in possession, remainder or reversion in at least 25% of the capital of the trust property • In the case of a trust not coming within (a), the class of individuals in whose main interest the trust is set up or operates • Any individual who has control over the trust. (s.28) (The requirement to identify and verify the beneficial ownership of a trust that arises pursuant to s.33 of the Act accords *inter alia* with the thirty-fourth of the FATF 40 Recommendations) (FATF, *FATF 40 Recommendations*, p.12).
ESTATE OF DECEASED PERSON IN ADMINISTRATION	• Executor or administrator (s.29).

OTHER ARRANGEMENT/ ENTITY THAT ADMINISTERS AND DISTRIBUTES FUNDS	• Any individual who benefits from at least 25% of the property of the arrangement or entity (if the individuals who benefit have been determined).
	• The class of individuals in whose main interest the entity or arrangement is set up or operates (if the individuals who benefit have yet to be determined).
	• Any individual who exercises control over at least 25% of the property of the entity or arrangement.
	• Any individual who is the beneficial owner of a body corporate that benefits from or exercises control over the property of the entity/arrangement is taken to benefit from or exercise control over the property of the entity/arrangement. (s.30)
ALL OTHER INSTANCES	• In relation to a case not covered by any of ss. 26, 27, 28, 29, 30(1), any individual who ultimately owns or controls a customer or on whose behalf a transaction is conducted. (s.30(3)).

Beneficial owner in relation to partnerships

27.—In this Part, "beneficial owner", in relation to a partnership, means any individual who—

(a) ultimately is entitled to or controls, whether the entitlement or control is direct or indirect, more than a 25 per cent share of the capital or profits of the partnership or more than 25 per cent of the voting rights in the partnership, or

(b) otherwise exercises control over the management of the partnership.

Beneficial owner in relation to trusts

28.—(1) In this section, "trust" means a trust that administers and distributes funds.

(2) In this Part, "beneficial owner", in relation to a trust, means any of the following:

(a) any individual who is entitled to a vested interest in possession, remainder or reversion, whether or not the interest is defeasible, in at least 25 per cent of the capital of the trust property;

(b) in the case of a trust other than one that is set up or operates entirely for the benefit of individuals referred to in *paragraph (a)*, the class of individuals in whose main interest the trust is set up or operates;

(c) any individual who has control over the trust.

(3) For the purposes of and without prejudice to the generality of *subsection (2)*, an individual who is the beneficial owner of a body corporate that—

(*a*) is entitled to a vested interest of the kind referred to in *subsection (2)(a)*, or

(*b*) has control over the trust,

is taken to be entitled to the vested interest or to have control over the trust (as the case may be).

(4) Except as provided by *subsection (5)*, in this section "control", in relation to a trust, means a power (whether exercisable alone, jointly with another person or with the consent of another person) under the trust instrument concerned or by law to do any of the following:

(*a*) dispose of, advance, lend, invest, pay or apply trust property;

(*b*) vary the trust;

(*c*) add or remove a person as a beneficiary or to or from a class of beneficiaries;

(*d*) appoint or remove trustees;

(*e*) direct, withhold consent to or veto the exercise of any power referred to in *paragraphs (a)* to *(d)*.

(5) For the purposes of the definition of "control" in *subsection (4)*, an individual does not have control solely as a result of the power exercisable collectively at common law to vary or extinguish a trust where the beneficiaries under the trust are at least 18 years of age, have full capacity and (taken together) are absolutely entitled to the property to which the trust applies.

Beneficial owner in relation to estates of deceased persons

29.—In this Part, "beneficial owner", in relation to an estate of a deceased person in the course of administration, means the executor or administrator of the estate concerned.

Other persons who are beneficial owners

30.—(1) In this Part, "beneficial owner", in relation to a legal entity or legal arrangement, other than where *section 26, 27* or *28*, applies, means—

(*a*) if the individuals who benefit from the entity or arrangement have been determined, any individual who benefit from at least 25 per cent of the property of the entity or arrangement,

(*b*) if the individuals who benefit from the entity or arrangement have yet to be determined, the class of such individuals in whose main interest the entity or arrangement is set up or operates, and

(*c*) any individual who exercises control over at least 25 per cent of the property of the entity or arrangement.

(2) For the purposes of and without prejudice to the generality of *subsection (1)*, any individual who is the beneficial owner of a body corporate that benefits from or exercises control over the property of the

entity or arrangement is taken to benefit from or exercise control over the property of the entity or arrangement.

(3) In this Part, "beneficial owner", in relation to a case other than a case to which *section 26, 27, 28* or *29*, or *subsection (1)* of this section, applies, means any individual who ultimately owns or controls a customer or on whose behalf a transaction is conducted.

(4) In this section, "arrangement" or "entity" means an arrangement or entity that administers and distributes funds.

CHAPTER 2

Designation of places other than Member States — procedures for detecting money laundering or terrorist financing

Designation of places imposing requirements equivalent to Third Money Laundering Directive

31.—(1) For the purposes of the definition of "acceptable institution" in *section 33* and its application in that section, the definition of "specified customers" in *section 34* and its application in that section and *section 36*, the definition of "relevant third party" in *section 40* and its application in that section, and for the purposes of *sections 34(2)(b)(ii), 51(2)* and *(3)* and *52(2)*, the Minister may, after consultation with the Minister for Finance, by order designate a place other than a Member State if the Minister is satisfied that the place imposes requirements equivalent to those specified in the Third Money Laundering Directive.

(2) The designation of a place other than a Member State under this section does not apply so long as the place is the subject of a decision adopted by the European Commission and in force, under Articles 40(4) and 41(2) of the Third Money Laundering Directive.

Section Note

Section 31 empowers the Minister for Justice and Law Reform, after consultation with the Minister for Finance, to designate, for the purposes of the provisions stated, a place other than Ireland if the Minister is satisfied that the place imposes requirements equivalent to those specified in the Directive. Under the Criminal Justice (Money Laundering and Terrorist Financing) Act 2010 (Section 31) Order 2010 (S.I. No. 343 of 2010) the following "places" have been designated for the purposes of s.31: Argentina; Australia; Brazil; Canada; Hong Kong; Iceland; Japan; Liechtenstein; Mexico; New Zealand; Norway; Russian Federation; Singapore; Switzerland; South Africa; the United States of America; the Channel Islands; the Isle of Man; the Dutch overseas territories of Netherlands Antilles and Aruba; and the French overseas territories of Mayotte, New Caledonia, French Polynesia, Saint Pierre and Miquelon and Wallis and Futuna. Notwithstanding that a place has been designated under s.31, such designation does not apply so long as the relevant place is the subject of a decision made by the European Commission and in force under Arts.40(4) and 41(2) of the

Directive. The reference to "places" in S.I. No. 343 of 2010 is of interest. If one looks, for example, to the (now revoked) Criminal Justice Act 1994 (Section 32(10)(d)) Regulations 1995 (S.I. No. 106 of 1995) these included, *inter alia*, "The Channel Islands" in a list of prescribed "states and countries" whereas neither the Channel Islands as a collective entity nor any of the islands which make up the Channel Islands is either a state or a country under international law. The reference to "The Channel Islands" as a "place" in S.I. 343 of 2010 is an improvement.

Deisgnation of places having inadequate procedures for detection of money laundering or terrorist financing

32.—(1) The Minister may, after consultation with the Minister for Finance, by order designate a place that is not a Member State, for the purposes of *sections 34(3)*, *36(2)* and *43*, if the Minister is satisfied that the place does not have adequate procedures in place for the detection of money laundering or terrorist financing.

(2) A place that is the subject of a decision adopted by the European Commission and in force, under Articles 40(4) and 41(2) of the Third Money Laundering Directive is taken to have been designated under this section.

CHAPTER 3

Customer Due Diligence

General Note

Chapter 3 of Pt.4 (ss.33 to 40) of the Act is concerned with customer due diligence (or "CDD"), in effect the identification and verification of customers and beneficial owners by designated persons. Chapter 3 contains the provisions that require, for example, credit institutions to undertake identity checks of persons seeking to open accounts with them. Section 33 identifies what CDD measures are to be taken by designated person, and when. Section 34 establishes certain exemptions from s.33. Section 35 makes certain special provision in respect of "business relationships". S.36 refines the application of s.35, establishing an exemption from s.35(1). Section 37 provides for enhanced CDD in respect of politically exposed persons. Section 38 provides for enhanced CDD in the context of correspondent banking relationships. Section 39 makes clear that designated persons retain a discretion to apply additional enhanced CDD, in particular where a designated person considers that there is a heightened risk of money laundering or terrorist financing. Section 40 makes provision as regards reliance by designated persons on third parties to do CDD. For a detailed consideration of the CDD requirements of the Act, see also Barrett, M., "Customer Identification under Ireland's new Anti-Money Laundering and Terrorist Financing Legislation", Parts I and II at [2010] J.I.B.L.R. 502 and 568.

Identification and verification of customers and beneficial owners

33.—(1) A designated person shall apply the measures specified in *subsections (2)* and, where applicable, *(4)*, in relation to a customer of the designated person—

(*a*) prior to establishing a business relationship with the customer,

(*b*) prior to carrying out an occasional transaction with, for or on behalf of the customer or assisting the customer to carry out an occasional transaction,

(*c*) prior to carrying out any service for the customer, if the person has reasonable grounds to believe that there is a real risk that the customer is involved in, or the service sought by the customer is for the purpose of, money laundering or terrorist financing, based on any of the following, or other, circumstances:

   (i)   the customer, or the type of customer, concerned;

   (ii) if the person has a business relationship with the customer, the type of business relationship concerned;

   (iii) the type of service or of any transaction or product in respect of which the service is sought;

   (iv) the purpose (or the customer's explanation of the purpose) of the service or of any transaction or product in respect of which the service is sought;

   (v) the value of any transaction or product in respect of which the service is sought;

   (vi) the source (or the customer's explanation of the source) of funds for any such transaction or product,

   or

(*d*) prior to carrying out any service for the customer if—

   (i) the person has reasonable grounds to doubt the veracity or adequacy of documents (whether or not in electronic form) or information that the person has previously obtained for the purpose of verifying the identity of the customer, whether obtained under this section or section 32 of the Criminal Justice Act 1994 ("the 1994 Act") prior to its repeal by this Act or under any administrative arrangements that the person may have applied before section 32 of the 1994 Act operated in relation to the person, and

   (ii) the person has not obtained any other documents or information that the person has reasonable grounds to believe can be relied upon to confirm the identity of the customer.

(2) The measures that shall be applied by a designated person under *subsection (1)* are as follows:

(*a*) identifying the customer, and verifying the customer's identity on the basis of documents (whether or not in electronic form), or information, that the designated person has reasonable grounds to believe can be relied upon to confirm the identity of the customer, including—

(i) documents from a government source (whether or not a State government source), or

(ii) any prescribed class of documents, or any prescribed combination of classes of documents;

(b) identifying any beneficial owner connected with the customer or service concerned, and taking measures reasonably warranted by the risk of money laundering or terrorist financing—

(i) to verify the beneficial owner's identity to the extent necessary to ensure that the person has reasonable grounds to be satisfied that the person knows who the beneficial owner is, and

(ii) in the case of a legal entity or legal arrangement of a kind referred to in *section 26, 27, 28* or *30*, to understand the ownership and control structure of the entity or arrangement concerned.

(3) Nothing in *subsection (2)(a)(i)* or *(ii)* limits the kinds of documents or information that a designated person may have reasonable grounds to believe can be relied upon to confirm the identity of a customer.

(4) Without prejudice to the generality of *subsection (2)(a)*, one or more of the following measures shall be applied by a designated person under *subsection (1)*, where a customer who is an individual does not present to the designated person for verification in person of the customer's identity:

(a) verification of the customer's identity on the basis of documents (whether or not in electronic form), or information, that the designated person has reasonable grounds to believe are reliable as confirmation of the identity of the customer in addition to any documents or information that would ordinarily have been used to verify the customer's identity if the customer had presented to the designated person for verification in person of the customer's identity;

(b) verification of documents supplied, for the purposes of verifying the identity of the customer under this section, to the designated person by the customer;

(c) verification of the customer's identity on the basis of confirmation received from an acceptable institution that the customer is, or has been, a customer of that institution;

(d) ensuring that one or more of the following transactions is carried out through an account in the customer's name with an acceptable institution that is a credit institution:

(i) the first payment made by the customer to the designated person for the provision of a service;

(ii) in the case of a designated person acting for or on behalf of the customer in respect of a financial transaction or a transaction relating to land, the first payment made by the customer in respect of the transaction;

(iii) in the case of a designated person that is another credit institution or is a financial institution, the first payment made by the customer to the designated person for the provision of a product;

(iv) in the case of a designated person that is another credit institution, the first occasion on which credit is received by the customer from the designated person or on which money is deposited with the designated person by the customer;

(v) in the case of a designated person trading in goods in respect of transactions involving payments as referred to in *section 25(1)(i)*, the first such payment made by the customer to the designated person.

(5) Notwithstanding *subsection (1)(a)*, a designated person may verify the identity of a customer or beneficial owner, in accordance with *subsections (2)* and, where applicable, *(4)*, during the establishment of a business relationship with the customer if the designated person has reasonable grounds to believe that—

(a) verifying the identity of the customer or beneficial owner (as the case may be) prior to the establishment of the relationship would interrupt the normal conduct of business, and

(b) there is no real risk that the customer is involved in, or the service sought by the customer is for the purpose of, money laundering or terrorist financing, but the designated person shall take reasonable steps to verify the identity of the customer or beneficial owner, in accordance with *subsections (2)* and, where applicable, *(4)*, as soon as practicable.

(6) Notwithstanding *subsection (1)(a)*, a credit institution may allow a bank account to be opened with it by a customer before verifying the identity of the customer or a beneficial owner, in accordance with *subsections (2)* and, where applicable, *(4)*, so long as the institution ensures that transactions in connection with the account are not carried out by or on behalf of the customer or beneficial owner before carrying out that verification.

(7) Notwithstanding *subsection (1)(a)*, a designated person may verify the identity of a beneficiary under a life assurance policy, in accordance with *subsections (2)* and, where applicable, *(4)*, after the business relationship concerned has been established, but the designated person shall carry out that verification before—

(a) the policy is paid out, or

(b) the beneficiary exercises any other right vested under the policy.

(8) A designated person who is unable to apply the measures specified in *subsection (2)* or *(4)* in relation to a customer, as a result of any failure on the part of the customer to provide the designated person with documents or information required under this section—

(a) shall not provide the service or carry out the transaction sought by that customer for so long as the failure remains unrectified, and

(b) shall discontinue the business relationship (if any) with the customer.

(9) Except as provided by *section 34*, a designated person who fails to comply with this section commits an offence and is liable—

(*a*) on summary conviction, to a fine not exceeding €5,000 or imprisonment for a term not exceeding 12 months (or both), or

(*b*) on conviction on indictment, to a fine or imprisonment for a term not exceeding 5 years (or both).

(10) In this section, "acceptable institution" means a credit institution or financial institution (other than an undertaking that is a financial institution solely because the undertaking provides either foreign exchange services or payment services, or both) that—

(*a*) carries on business in the State as a designated person,

(*b*) is situated in another Member State and supervised or monitored for compliance with requirements specified in the Third Money Laundering Directive, in accordance with Section 2 of Chapter V of that Directive, or

(*c*) is situated in a place designated under *section 31* and supervised or monitored in the place for compliance with requirements equivalent to those specified in the Third Money Laundering Directive.

(11) The Minister may prescribe a class of documents, or a combination of classes of documents, for the purposes of *subsection (2)(a)(ii)*, only if the Minister is satisfied that the class or combination of documents would be adequate to verify the identity of customers of designated persons.

(12) For the purposes of *subsection (2)(a)(ii)*, the Minister may prescribe different classes of documents, or combinations of classes of documents, for different kinds of designated persons, customers, transactions, services or risks of money laundering or terrorist financing.

Section Note
Overview

Section 33(1) provides when a designated person shall apply the CDD measures specified in s.33(2) and (4), thus "prior to establishing a business relationship with the customer" (s.33(1)(a)), "prior to carrying out an occasional transaction" (s.33(1)(b)), and, in certain instances, "prior to carrying out any service for the customer" (s.33(1)(c)). (The term "occasional transaction" is defined in s.24(1)). It is worth noting that for a person to be a customer of a designated person does not require that there be any "business relationship" (within the meaning of the Act) between the designated person and the customer; indeed it is apparent from the definition of "business relationship" that a person will already have been a customer before a "business relationship" is established. All of this suggests that a customer relationship is established at a very early stage, likely from the moment that a customer puts, and perhaps from the moment that the customer approaches a designated person with a view to putting, his custom with that designated person, making compliance with s.33(1) a matter that must generally be complied with at a very early stage of the 'supplier-customer' relationship. Section 33(5) allows for CDD to occur during the establishment of (*i.e.* not prior to establishing) a business relationship in defined instances. Section 33(6), subject to various constraints, allows a credit institution to open a "bank account" before CDD has been undertaken. The reference to a "bank account" is perhaps unfortunate in that logically it would seem that only a bank can allow a "bank account" to be opened with it and thus a question perhaps arises as to whether s.33(6), though expressed to apply to credit institutions, is in fact constrained by its own terms so that it only applies to banks. (This apparent anomaly derives from Art.9(4) of the Directive which likewise provides that by way of derogation from *e.g.* the general requirement that verification of identity take place before the establishment of a business relationship or the carrying out of a transaction "Member States may allow the opening of a bank account provided that there are adequate safeguards in place to ensure that transactions are not carried out by the customer or on its behalf until full compliance with the aforementioned provisions is obtained". As Art.9(4) establishes a derogation from Arts.9(1) and (2) of the Directive it would have been an expansion of this derogation, and hence a lightening of the requirements established by the Directive, for s.33(6) of the Act to refer to any account other than a "bank account". Whereas Ireland could, pursuant to Art.5 of the Directive, have adopted or retained in place a provision of domestic law stricter than the Directive requires, it was not open to Ireland to lighten the requirements of the Directive). Section 33(7) permits a designated person, in defined circumstances, to verify the identity of a beneficiary under a life assurance policy after a business relationship has been established with such beneficiary. The requirements of s.33 are summarised in Diagram 3 below. Certain aspects of s.33 are further amplified upon hereafter. The various identification and verification requirements in

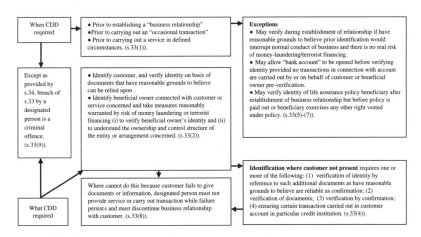

Diagram 3. CDD under s.33

the Act largely accord with the requirements of the fifth of the FATF 40 Recommendations (see FATF, *FATF 40 Recommendations*, p.4).

Section 33(1)
Section 33(1) requires that a designated person undertake CDD in relation to a customer of a designated person:

(a) *prior to establishing a business relationship with the customer (s.33(1)(a))*

Section 24(1) defines the term "business relationship" as meaning "in relation to a designated person and a customer of that person...a business, professional or commercial relationship between the person and the customer that the person expects to be ongoing". Offhand it would seem possible for a designated person to seek to frustrate or delay a prosecution for breach of s.33(1)(a) simply by claiming that at the time of the alleged breach it did not expect the relationship between it and the relevant customer to be ongoing.

The difference between "prior to establishing", as referred to in s.33(1)(a) and "during the establishment of", as referred to in s.33(5) is perhaps narrower than may appear on an initial reading. Thus "prior to establishing" appears to embrace the period up to but not including the moment of establishment. The term "during the establishment of" appears to embrace the period up to but not beyond the moment of establishment.

(b) *prior to carrying out an occasional transaction with, for or on behalf of the customer or assisting the customer to carry out an occasional transaction (s.33(1)(b))*

The term "occasional transaction" is defined in s.24(1) of the Act as meaning "in relation to a customer of a designated person...a single transaction, or a series of transactions that are or appear to be linked to each other, where – (a) the designated person does not have a business relationship with the customer, and (b) the total amount of money paid by the customer in the single transaction or series is greater than €15,000". As mentioned above, the term "customer" is given a relatively limited definition in s.24(1). However, it is clear from the definition of "business relationship" that a customer relationship may arise relatively quickly for the purposes of the Act between a supplier and a customer. This is because a "business relationship" (which itself arises when a designated person expects a business, professional or commercial relationship with a customer to be ongoing) is predicated on there already being a customer relationship in place. As such an expectation can be formed relatively quickly, this suggests that a customer relationship can be formed even more quickly. It would seem prudent to assume that a person becomes a customer at the moment that such person places custom with a supplier and it is at least conceivable that a customer relationship could be found to arise where a person approaches a supplier with a view to placing custom with that supplier. Consequently s.33(1)(b) may be of wider ambit than at first glance appears.

(c) *prior to carrying out any service for the customer, if the designated person has reasonable grounds to believe that there is a real risk that the customer is involved in, or the service sought by the customer is for the purpose of, money laundering or terrorist financing, by reference to certain defined circumstances "or other" circumstances (i.e. the circumstances defined are not exhaustive) (s.33(1)(c))*

The Act does not indicate what constitute "reasonable grounds". Nor does it indicate what constitutes a "real risk", though a natural reading of this last phrase suggests that something more substantial than a mere risk is required. Consistent with the risk-based approach to compliance adopted by the Directive, the non-definition of these terms gives designated persons some flexibility to decide how best to proceed, though in practice it is possible that designated persons may consider their freedom of action constrained in this regard by reference to any guidelines approved under section 107 of the Act and/or the extent to which the competent authority responsible for monitoring the relevant designated person considers rigorous compliance with any (if any) applicable approved guidelines to be, in effect, mandatory practice. (On competent authorities, see further the consideration of Chapter 8 of Part 4 below). Notably, this provision is both customer-focused and service-focused, *i.e.* it applies where a designated person has reasonable grounds to believe that there is a real risk either that a customer is involved in money laundering or terrorist financing or that the service sought by the customer is for the purpose of money laundering or terrorist financing. Among the circumstances referred to in s.33(1)(c) are (at (iv)) "the purpose (or the customer's explanation of the purpose of the service or of any transaction or product in respect of which the service is sought" and (at (vi)) "the source (or the customer's explanation of the source) of funds for any such transaction or product". A person seeking, for example, to commit the offence of money laundering is likely of course to be extremely terse as to the matters aforesaid or simply to lie in this regard.

(d) *prior to carrying out any service for the customer if the designated person has reasonable grounds to doubt the veracity or adequacy of documents or information obtained for CDD purposes under the anti-money laundering regime established by the Criminal Justice Act 1994 or previous administrative arrangements, and the designated person has not obtained any other documents or information that the designated person has reasonable grounds to believe can be relied upon to confirm the identity of the customer (s.33(1)(d))*

Given that, save in certain defined instances, breach of s.33 is an offence, the practical effect of this requirement would seem to be that, to avoid a contravention of s.33(1)(d), designated persons should, on a rolling basis, consider whether they are satisfied as to the veracity or adequacy of the documents or information referred to above, so as to take account of any new facts of which the designated person may become aware from time to time. The Act does not indicate what constitute "reasonable grounds" thus giving a designated person some freedom in this regard (albeit that this freedom entails the risk of getting matters wrong).

Section 33(2) to (4)
As mentioned above s.33(1) (and s.33(5), (6) and (7), considered hereafter) are concerned with the issue as to when CDD must be undertaken by designated persons. S.33(2) to (4) is concerned with what and how CDD must be undertaken.

Section 33(2)
Section 33(2) imposes a twofold obligation whereby a customer/beneficial owner must be identified and that identity must also be verified. S.33(2)(a) provides that the measures to be applied by a designated person pursuant to s.33(1) comprise: identifying a customer and verifying customer identity on the basis of documents or information that the designated person has "reasonable grounds" to believe can be relied upon to confirm customer identity; and identifying any beneficial owner connected with a customer/service and taking measures "reasonably warranted" by the risk of money laundering or terrorist financing (a) to verify the beneficial owner's identity to the extent necessary to ensure that the designated person has "reasonable grounds" to be satisfied as to who the beneficial owner is, and (b) in the case of certain defined legal entities or arrangements, to understanding their ownership or control structure. Again, consistent with the risk-based approach to compliance anticipated by the Directive, the non-definition of the quoted terms gives designated persons some flexibility to decide how best to proceed, subject perhaps to what any approved guidelines may provide and how any applicable approved guidelines are interpreted by competent authorities.

Section 33(3)
Section 33(3) makes clear that s.33(2)(a) in referring to various documents does not mean to constrain those documents or information that a designated person may have reasonable grounds to believe can be relied upon to confirm customer identity.

Section 33(4)
Recital (14) to the Directive states that the Directive "should also apply to those activities of the institutions and persons covered hereunder which are performed on the Internet". Section 33(4) makes special provision regarding the CDD measures to be applied where a designated person does not meet a customer in person. A good example of where this might occur in practice is with an online bank that does not maintain a branch network. Another possible example would be telephone banking. Because of the heightened risk of fraud and impersonation in such circumstances, s.33(4) of the Act establishes a variety of identity verification measures, one or more of which must be applied where a customer who is an individual (a natural person), does not present to the designated person for verification in person of his or her identity. Section 33(4) is consistent with the eighth of the FATF 40 Recommendations which states that

> "Financial institutions should pay special attention to any money laundering threats that may arise from new or developing technologies that might favour anonymity. ...In particular, financial institutions should have policies and procedures in place to address any specific risks associated with non-face to face business relationships or transactions."" (FATF, *FATF 40 Recommendations*, p.6).

(There is, of course, also a blanket prohibition on anonymous accounts in s.58 of the Act).

Section 33(4)(a) The documents that a designated person has "reasonable grounds" to believe are reliable as confirmation of customer identity could helpfully be amplified upon in any guidelines approved under s.107 of the Act.

Section 33(4)(c) It is perhaps questionable whether in practice a confirmation under s.33(4)(c) of the Act will come without qualification (and whether in the presence of such qualification it would be safe to rely upon same).

Section 33(4)(d) In practice, any prudent online bank seems likely to insist that the initial flow of funds on an account with it come within one of the categories identified in s.33(4)(d), thus effectively obviating the need for further verification of customer identity above and beyond that required by s.33(2) of the Act.

Section 33(5) to (7)

Section 33(5), (6) and (7) somewhat ameliorate the requirements of s.33(1) by recognising that undertaking CDD as early
as s.33(1) requires may not always be practically feasible. Thus
s.33(5) allows for CDD to occur during (*i.e.* not prior to) the
establishment of a business relationship in defined instances.
Section 33(6), subject to various constraints, allows a credit
institution to open a "bank account" before CDD has been
undertaken. (The implications of the reference to a "bank
account" have been considered in the overview of s.33 above).
Section 33(6) faithfully implements Art.9(4) of the Directive but
both provisions appear not entirely consistent with the fifth of the
FATF Recommendations which provides, *inter alia*, that:

> "Where the financial institution is unable to comply with
> [the due diligence requirements referred elsewhere in the
> recommendation], it should not open the account." (FATF,
> *FATF 40 Recommendations*, p.4).

The effect of s.33(6) (and Art.9(4)) is that an account can be
opened (it just cannot be operated until verification of customer/
beneficial owner identity is complete).

Section 33(5) The exception established by s.33(5) of the Act to
the general obligation imposed by s.33(1) of the Act on
designated persons to undertake CDD in respect of a customer
prior to establishing a business relationship with a customer is
relatively narrow and so caveated that a question perhaps arises
as to whether it ought to be much relied upon in practice. Section
33(5) allows a designated person to *verify* the identity of a
customer or beneficial owner, in accordance with s.33(2) and
(where applicable) s.33(4), during the establishment of a business relationship in certain defined circumstances. It will be
recalled that s.33(2) requires a designated person both to identify
a customer/beneficial owner and also to verify that identity. The
exception established by s.33(5) applies only to verification of
identity. In addition, the exception only applies if the designated
person has "reasonable grounds" to believe that (a) in effect,
conforming with s.33(1)(a) would interrupt "the normal conduct of
business" and also (b) there is no "real risk" (the phrase is not
defined but presumably means to refer to something more
substantial than a mere risk) that the customer is involved in or
the service sought by the customer is for the purpose of money
laundering or terrorist financing. Apart altogether from the issues
of when a designated person may prudently consider itself to
have "reasonable grounds" and what exactly constitutes "the
normal conduct of business" and/or a "real risk", there is perhaps
another more fundamental difficulty with the s.33(5) exception.
This arises from the definition of the term "business relationship".

It will be recalled that the term "business relationship" is defined in s.24(1) as meaning, in relation to a designated person and a customer of that person, a business, professional or commercial relationship between the person and the customer that the designated person expects to be ongoing. If a designated person has identified a customer and is, for example, entering into various commercial negotiations with that customer prior to that customer's identity being verified, it seems likely that the designated person has already crossed the threshold of expecting the relationship between it and that customer to be ongoing, *i.e.* it seems likely already to be in a business relationship. However, the exception established by s.33(5) only applies during the establishment of a business relationship (a period of time which would appear to extend up to but not beyond the moment that a business relationship is established). Thereafter it would appear that a customer must have been identified and that identity verified unless another exception applies. What all of this means is that the window of opportunity to rely upon the s.33(5) exception is very narrow, perhaps too narrow ever safely to be relied upon. Further constraining the usefulness of s.33(5) in this regard is that even if a designated person elects to rely upon the exception established thereby, the designated person must take reasonable steps to verify the identity of the relevant customer/beneficial owner "as soon as practicable". The length of time after a customer relationship is established but before a "business relationship" arises and also before it is practicable to verify the identity of that customer seems likely to be quite limited in duration, sufficiently so to raise a question as to whether s.33(5) can ever safely be relied upon, especially given that breach of s.33 is, save in certain defined instances, a criminal offence.

Section 33(6) A potential difficulty with s.33(6) has already been identified in the overview of section 33 above, namely that it allows an exception to the requirements of s.33(1)(a) where a credit institution allows a "bank account" to be opened with it. However, it would seem that only a bank can allow a bank account to be opened with it and thus a question arises as to whether the exception established by s.33(6) can be availed of by any credit institution other than a bank.

Section 33(7) Section 33(7) permits a designated person, in defined circumstances, to verify the identity of a beneficiary under a life assurance policy after a business relationship has been established with such beneficiary.

Section 33(8) Section 33(8) makes sense when viewed in the light of a new business relationship in that it is a relatively straightforward matter, for example, for a credit institution to refuse to provide any service to, or engage in anything but the most cursory of dealings with, a customer until that customer has provided the documentation necessary for the credit institution to discharge its CDD obligations under s.33. Offhand, compliance with s.33(8) may present practical difficulties in respect of an existing business relationship. It will be recalled that under s.33(1)(d) an identification and verification obligation arises prior to carrying out a service for a customer where, in essence, there are reasonable grounds for a designated person to doubt the veracity or adequacy of CDD documents or information previously obtained and no supplementary documents or information are obtained to confirm customer identity. It is conceivable that an internal audit or compliance check within an entity that is a designated person could identify that certain CDD documentation obtained as standard by that institution from customers by reference to applicable guidance notes or guidelines was not obtained in the past. It is also conceivable that the relevant customer may by that time have gone abroad for a prolonged period of time but continues, for example, to arrange for repayment of an existing loan with that designated person either from within Ireland or from abroad. If such customer proves, understandably, to be uncontactable and no other documents or information can be sourced so as to confirm the identity of the customer, s.33(8) appears to rely the cessation of all dealings with that customer even though, in the example given, the loan is being repaid and the deficiency in the CDD documentation may be more formal than real. The extent to which form will be allowed to triumph over substance in such instances seems likely to be strongly influenced by the approach taken by "competent authorities" (within the meaning of Ch.8 of Pt.4) in this regard when discharging their obligations under s.63 of the Act.

Section 33(9) Except as provided by s.34, failure by a designated person to comply with s.33 is an offence. See further the table of offences arising under the Act (and the penalties for same) in Appendix 2 of this text.

Exemptions from *section 33*

34.—(1) A designated person is not required to apply the measures specified in *section 33(2)* if the customer or product concerned is a specified customer or specified product, as the case may be.

(2) A credit institution is not required to apply the measures specified in *section 33(2)(b)* in respect of the beneficial ownership of money held, or proposed to be held, in trust—

(*a*) in a client account, within the meaning of the Solicitors (Amendment) Act 1994, or (*b*) in an account for clients of a person who by way of business, provides legal or notarial services to those clients—

    (i) in a Member State and who is supervised or monitored for compliance with requirements specified in the Third Money Laundering Directive, in accordance with Section 2 of Chapter V of that Directive, or

    (ii) in a place that is designated under *section 31* and who is supervised or monitored in the place for compliance with requirements equivalent to those specified in the Third Money Laundering Directive.

(3) A designated person shall not apply the exemptions provided for in *subsections (1)* and *(2)* in any of the following circumstances:

    (*a*) the customer concerned is from a place that is designated under *section 32*;

    (*b*) *section 33(1)(c)* or *(d)* or *(4)* applies;

    (*c*) the designated person is required to apply measures, in relation to the customer or beneficial owner (if any) concerned, under *section 37*.

(4) A credit institution may apply the exemption provided for in *subsection (2)* in relation to the beneficial ownership of money held in trust in a credit institution only if the credit institution is satisfied that information on the identity of the beneficial owners of the money held in the account is available, on request, to the credit institution.

(5) For the purposes of this section, a specified customer is—

    (*a*) a credit institution or financial institution that—

        (i)   carries on business in the State as a designated person,

        (ii) is situated in another Member State and supervised or monitored for compliance with requirements laid down in the Third Money Laundering Directive, in accordance with Section 2 of Chapter V of that Directive, or

        (iii) is situated in a place designated under *section 31* and supervised or monitored in the place for compliance with requirements equivalent to those laid down in the Third Money Laundering Directive,

    (*b*) a listed company whose securities are admitted to trading on a regulated market,

    (*c*) a public body, or

    (*d*) a body (whether incorporated or unincorporated) that—

        (i)   has been entrusted with public functions under a provision of the treaties of the European Communities or under an Act adopted by an institution of the European Communities,

        (ii) in the reasonable opinion of the designated person concerned, the identity of the body is publicly available, transparent and certain,

        (iii) in the reasonable opinion of the designated person concerned, the activities of the body and its accounting practices are transparent, and

        (iv) the body is either accountable to an institution of the European Communities or to a public authority of a Member State.

(6) A reference in *subsection (5)* to a financial institution does not include a reference to an undertaking that is a financial institution solely because the undertaking provides either foreign exchange services or payment services, or both.

(7) For the purposes of this section, a specified product is—

(*a*) a life assurance policy having an annual premium of no more than €1,000 or a single premium of no more than €2,500,

(*b*) an insurance policy in respect of a pension scheme, being a policy that does not have a surrender clause and may not be used as collateral,

(*c*) a pension, superannuation or similar scheme that provides for retirement benefits to employees and where contributions to the scheme are made by deductions from wages and the rules of the scheme do not permit a member's interest under the scheme to be assigned, or

(*d*) electronic money, within the meaning of the Electronic Money Directive, where—

    (i) in a case where the electronic device concerned cannot be recharged, the monetary value that may be stored electronically on the device does not exceed €250 or, if the device cannot be used outside of the State, €500, or

    (ii) in a case where the electronic device concerned can be recharged—

        (I) the total monetary value of all amounts by which the device may be charged or recharged (or both), in any calendar year, including any initial stored value of the device on purchase if the device is purchased during the year, does not exceed €2,500, and

        (II) none, or less than €1,000, of the electronic money may be redeemed by the issuer (as referred to in Article 11 of that Directive) in that year.

Section Note

Under s.33(9) of the Act, "except as provided by section 34" a designated person who fails to comply with s.33 is guilty of an offence. Section 34 in effect establishes two differing exemptions from the requirements of s.33. The first exemption applies to all designated persons. The second exemption applies to credit institutions only. The first exemption arises where the relevant customer or product is a "specified customer" or "specified product" (s.34(1)). What constitutes a "specified customer" or "specified product" is defined in s.34(5) (as supplemented by s.34(6)) and s.34(7) respectively. The various persons who constitute a "specified customer" are low-risk entities such as public bodies. The term "specified product" is identified in s.34(7) and embraces an array of low-risk products. Because of the low risk of money laundering or terrorist financing arising in respect of a "specified customer" or a "specified product" a designated person is not required to apply any of the measures specified in s.33(2) if a customer/product comes within the category of "specified customer"/"specified product", as appropriate. The second exemption arises as regards the beneficial ownership of money held, or proposed to be held, in trust (a) in a solicitor's client account or (b) certain similar client accounts of certain persons who, by way of business, provide legal or notarial services, to those clients (s.34(2)). Credit institutions need not apply the requirements of s.33(2)(b) in respect of the beneficial ownership of such monies. Section 33(2)(b) is concerned, *inter alia*, with the identification and verification of beneficial owners). Although the rationale for this second category of exceptions is not stated in the Act it is presumably because solicitors and such other persons as are mentioned are subject to their own regulatory regimes as regards the operation of client accounts and this renders it unnecessary to impose via the Act a further obligation to determine the beneficial owners of the monies in such accounts. As to s.34(4), it is perhaps questionable whether it would be prudent for a credit institution to place itself in a situation where it does not possess information necessary to demonstrate compliance with (or here avail of an exemption under) the Act but relies on another person producing same to it on request, even if that person is another company within the same group of companies.

Special measures applying to business relationships

35.—(1) A designated person shall obtain information reasonably warranted by the risk of money laundering or terrorist financing on the purpose and intended nature of a business relationship with a customer prior to the establishment of the relationship.

(2) A designated person who is unable to obtain such information, as a result of any failure on the part of the customer, shall not provide the service sought by the customer for so long as the failure continues.

(3) A designated person shall monitor dealings with a customer with whom the person has a business relationship, including (to the extent reasonably warranted by the risk of money laundering or terrorist financing) by scrutinising transactions and the source of wealth or of funds for those transactions, to determine whether or not the transactions are consistent with—

(a) the person's knowledge of the customer and the customer's business and pattern of transactions, and

(b) any knowledge that the person may have that the customer may be involved in money laundering or terrorist financing.

(4) Except as provided by *section 36*, a designated person who fails to comply with this section commits an offence and is liable—

(a) on summary conviction, to a fine not exceeding €5,000 or imprisonment for a term not exceeding 12 months (or both), or

(*b*) on conviction on indictment, to a fine or imprisonment for a term not exceeding 5 years (or both).

Section Note

It will be recalled that, for the purposes of Pt.4 of the Act, the term "business relationship" means "in relation to a designated person and a customer of the person...a business, professional or commercial relationship between the person and the customer that the [designated] person expects to be ongoing. (Per s.24(1)). Section 35(1) creates an additional obligation in the context of a business relationship whereby a designated person must not just identify and verify the identity of its customer (pursuant to s.33, *etc.*) but must obtain information "reasonably warranted" by the risk of money laundering or terrorist financing on the purpose and intended nature of a business relationship with that customer prior to the establishment of the relationship. Just what information is "reasonably warranted" could usefully be amplified upon in any guidelines approved under s.107 of the Act. Section 35(3) establishes a quite onerous monitoring obligation for designated persons and, at least in the case of high street credit institutions (insofar as scrutinising transactions is concerned) effectively requires them to have sophisticated computer software in place that highlight transactions which may present a money laundering or terrorist financing risk, with the final assessment as to whether in the particular circumstances of an individual customer they in fact present such a risk typically being left to members of the relevant institution's fraud and/or compliance teams to determine. This monitoring obligation accords with the eleventh of the FATF 40 Recommendations (see FATF, *FATF 40 Recommendations*, p. 7). Although the obligation to scrutinise transactions and the source of wealth or funds for same arises only "to the extent reasonably warranted by the risk of money laundering or terrorist financing" (per s.35(3)), the fact that failure by a designated person to comply with s.35 is (per s.35(4) and except as provided in s.36) a criminal offence, would suggest that designated persons, if they err at all, are perhaps likely err in favour of over-scrutiny. (On offences generally, see the table of offences arising under the Act (and the penalties for same) in Appendix 2 of this text).

Exemption from *section 35(1)*

36.—(1) A designated person is not required to comply with *section 35(1)* if the designated person has reasonable grounds for believing that the customer or product concerned is a specified customer or specified product, as the case may be.

(2) The exemption provided for in *subsection (1)* does not apply to a designated person in any of the following circumstances:

(*a*) the customer concerned is from a place that is designated under *section 32*;
(*b*) *section 33(1)(c)* or *(d)* or *(4)* applies;

(c) a designated person is required to apply measures, in relation to the customer or beneficial owner (if any) concerned, under *section 37*.

(3) For the purposes of this section, "specified customer" and "specified product" have the same meanings as they have in *section 34*.

Section Note

It is perhaps open to question whether a designated person who or which fell afoul of s.35 could bring itself outside the ambit of that provision simply by claiming that it did not expect the relevant customer relationship to be ongoing. However the only express exemption from the application of s.35(1) is that contained in s.36, *i.e.* where a designated person has reasonable grounds for believing that the relevant customer/product is a (low-risk) specified customer or is a (low-risk) specified product. Per s.36(3), the terms "specified customer" and "specified product" have the same meaning as is given those terms in s.34 (considered above). The instances referred to in s.36(2) mirror those referred to in s.34(3) (in which the scope of an exemption is likewise constrained).

Enhanced customer due diligence – politically exposed persons

37.—(1) A designated person shall take steps to determine whether or not a customer, or a beneficial owner connected with the customer or service concerned, being a customer or beneficial owner residing in a place outside the State, is a politically exposed person or an immediate family member, or a close associate of, a politically exposed person.

(2) The designated person shall take the steps prior to—

(a) establishing a business relationship with the customer, or

(b) carrying out an occasional transaction with, for or on behalf of the customer or assisting the customer to carry out an occasional transaction.

(3) The steps to be taken are such steps as are reasonably warranted by the risk that the customer or beneficial owner (as the case may be) is involved in money laundering or terrorist financing.

(4) If a designated person knows or has reasonable grounds to believe that a customer residing in a place outside the State is a politically exposed person or an immediate family member or close associate of a politically exposed person, the designated person shall—

(a) ensure that approval is obtained from any senior management of the designated person before a business relationship is established with the customer, and

(b) determine the source of wealth and of funds for the following transactions—

> (i) transactions the subject of any business relationship with the customer that are carried out with the customer or in respect of which a service is sought, or
>
> (ii) any occasional transaction that the designated person carries out with, for or on behalf of the customer or that the designated person assists the customer to carry out.

(5) Notwithstanding *subsections (2)(a)* and *(4)(a),* a credit institution may allow a bank account to be opened with it by a customer before taking the steps referred to in *subsection (1)* or seeking the approval referred to in *subsection (4)(a),* so long as the institution ensures that transactions in connection with the account are not carried out by or on behalf of the customer or any beneficial owner concerned before taking the steps or seeking the approval, as the case may be.

(6) If a designated person knows or has reasonable grounds to believe that a beneficial owner residing in a place outside the State, and connected with a customer or with a service sought by a customer, is a politically exposed person or an immediate family member or close associate of a politically exposed person, the designated person shall apply the measures specified in *subsection (4)(a)* and *(b)* in relation to the customer concerned.

(7) For the purposes of *subsections (4)* and *(6),* a designated person is deemed to know that another person is a politically exposed person or an immediate family member or close associate of a politically exposed person if, on the basis of—

> (a) information in the possession of the designated person (whether obtained under *subsections (1)* to *(3)* or otherwise),
>
> (b) in a case where the designated person has contravened *subsection (1)* or *(2),* information that would have been in the possession of the person if the person had complied with that provision, or
>
> (c) public knowledge, there are reasonable grounds for concluding that the designated person so knows.

(8) A designated person who is unable to apply the measures specified in *subsection (1), (3), (4)* or *(6)* in relation to a customer, as a result of any failure on the part of the customer to provide the designated person with documents or information—

> (a) shall discontinue the business relationship (if any) with the customer for so long as the failure continues, and
>
> (b) shall not provide the service or carry out the transaction sought by the customer for so long as the failure continues.

(9) A person who fails to comply with this section commits an offence and is liable—

(*a*) on summary conviction, to a fine not exceeding €5,000 or imprisonment for a term not exceeding 12 months (or both), or

(*b*) on conviction on indictment, to a fine or imprisonment for a term not exceeding 5 years (or both).

(10) In this section—

"close associate" of a politically exposed person includes any of the following persons:

(*a*) any individual who has joint beneficial ownership of a legal entity or legal arrangement, or any other close business relations, with the politically exposed person;

(*b*) any individual who has sole beneficial ownership of a legal entity or legal arrangement set up for the actual benefit of the politically exposed person;

"immediate family member" of a politically exposed person includes any of the following persons:

(*a*) any spouse of the politically exposed person;

(*b*) any person who is considered to be equivalent to a spouse of the politically exposed person under the national or other law of the place where the person or politically exposed person resides;

(*c*) any child of the politically exposed person;

(*d*) any spouse of a child of the politically exposed person;

(*e*) any person considered to be equivalent to a spouse of a child of the politically exposed person under the national or other law of the place where the person or child resides;

(*f*) any parent of the politically exposed person;

(*g*) any other family member of the politically exposed person who is of a prescribed class;

"politically exposed person" means an individual who is, or has at any time in the preceding 12 months been, entrusted with a prominent public function, including either of the following individuals (but not including any middle ranking or more junior official):

(*a*) a specified official;

(*b*) a member of the administrative, management or supervisory body of a state-owned enterprise;

"specified official" means any of the following officials (including any such officials in an institution of the European Communities or an international body):

(*a*) a head of state, head of government, government minister or deputy or assistant government minister;

(*b*) a member of a parliament;

(*c*) a member of a supreme court, constitutional court or other high level judicial body whose decisions, other than in exceptional circumstances, are not subject to further appeal;

(*d*) a member of a court of auditors or of the board of a central bank;

(*e*) an ambassador, chargé d'affairs or high-ranking officer in the armed forces.

(11) The Minister may prescribe a class of family member of a politically exposed person, for the purposes of *paragraph (g)* of the definition of "immediate family member" of a politically exposed person in *subsection (10)*, only if the Minister is satisfied that it would be appropriate for the provisions of this section to be applied in relation to members of the class, having regard to any heightened risk, arising from their close family relationship with the politically exposed person, that such members may be involved in money launderingor terrorist financing.

Section Note

Section 37, which accords with the sixth of the FATF 40 Recommendations (see FATF, *FATF 40 Recommendations*, p.5), is among the provisions of the Act that have attracted most attention. It is perhaps worth summarising the effect of the various elements of what is a lengthy provision:

- Section 37(1) requires a designated person to take steps to determine whether a customer or beneficial owner (connected with the customer or service concerned) residing in a place outside Ireland is (a) a politically exposed person, (b) an immediate family member of a politically exposed person, or (c) a close associate of a politically exposed person. Section 37(1) does not require that the customer or beneficial owner be ordinarily resident outside Ireland, merely that they be resident outside Ireland, which would appear at first glance to bring a wider array of persons within s.37(1) than would be the case if ordinary residence was the basis on which it applied. Although the customer or beneficial owner must be resident outside Ireland, there is no requirement that a politically exposed person of which a customer or beneficial owner is an immediate family member or close associate need be resident outside Ireland.

- Section 37(2) requires that the said steps be undertaken prior to establishing a business relationship with the customer and also when carrying out an occasional transaction with, for or on behalf of the customer or when assisting the customer to carry out an occasional transaction. It will be recalled that the term "occasional transaction" is a defined term (defined in s.24(1)).

- Section 37(3) provides that the steps to be taken are such as are "reasonably warranted" by the risk that the customer or beneficial owner (as applicable) is involved in money laundering or terrorist financing. The Act does not amplify further on what steps may be "reasonably warranted"; any guidelines approved under s.107 could usefully amplify on the meaning of this term.

- Section 37(4) requires that if a designated person knows "or has reasonable grounds" to believe that a customer residing in a place outside Ireland is a politically exposed person (or an immediate family member or close associate of same) the designated person must do two things: first, ensure that approval is obtained from any "senior management" of the designated person before a business relationship is established with the customer; second, determine the source of wealth and funds for certain prescribed transactions. The Act does not define what constitute "reasonable grounds" to believe that a particular customer is a politically exposed person or an immediate family member or close associate of same. The Act also does not define what constitutes "senior management". In the context of a credit institution the term would appear to refer, for example, to a branch manager upwards. However recital (26) to the Directive states in this regard that "Obtaining approval from senior management for establishing business relationships should not imply obtaining approval from the board of directors but from the immediate higher level of the hierarchy of the person seeking such approval". Given that in a credit institution an account can often be opened by counter staff the "immediate higher level of the hierarchy", were one to apply the standard identified in recital (26), potentially could be a relatively junior staff member.

- Section 37(5) permits a credit institution to allow a "bank account" to be opened with it provided no transactions in connection with the account are carried out by or on behalf of the relevant customer (or any beneficial owner) before the steps referred to above are taken or the above-mentioned senior management approval sought, as applicable. Again, the wording of this provision (like that of s.33(6), considered above) is notable in that it refers to a credit institution allowing a bank account to be opened with it, whereas logic suggests that only a bank can allow a bank account to be opened with it and thus s.37(5) appears, on its own terms, to be constrained in application to accounts with banks only.

- Section 37(6) makes provision in respect of beneficial owners, requiring a designated person to apply the measures referred to therein in relation to a customer (who may be a customer in Ireland) where the designated person knows or believes a beneficial owner residing in a place outside Ireland and connected with the customer (or with a service sought by the customer) is a politically exposed person, an immediate family member of a politically exposed person or a close associate of a politically exposed person. It is not clear what criteria are to be applied in determining whether a beneficial owner is "connected with" a customer or a service sought by a customer.

- Section 37(7) provides that a designated person is deemed to know that another person is a politically exposed person, an immediate family member of a politically exposed person or a close associate of a politically exposed person if, on the basis of certain information that is or ought to have been in the possession of that designated person or on the basis of public knowledge (presumably, though this is not stated, Irish public knowledge) there are reasonable grounds for concluding that the person so knows.
- Section 37(8) provides that where a designated person is unable to undertake enhanced CDD in relation to a customer as a result of any failure by the customer to provide documents or information to the designated person, the designated person must discontinue any (if any) business relationship with that customer for so long as the failure continues and must not provide the service or carry out the transaction sought by the customer for so long as the failure continues.
- Section 37(9) provides that failure to comply with s.37 is a criminal offence. (See generally the table of offences arising under the Act (and the penalties for same) in Appendix 2 of this text).
- Section 37(10) defines the terms "politically exposed person", Immediate family member", "close associate" and "specified official". Some comments on certain of these definitions follow.

"politically exposed person"
The term "prominent public function" is not defined in the Act, nor is there any attempt made to clarify what constitutes a "middle ranking or more junior official". The Directive refers in its definition of the term "politically exposed persons" (in Article 3(8)) to natural persons who are or have been entrusted with "prominent public functions" and though this latter term is not defined in the Directive, section 2(2) of the Act applies and the almost identical expression in the Act can be taken to enjoy the same meaning in the Act as that term may be determined to enjoy in the Directive.

"immediate family member"
The categories of person referred to at parts (b) and (e) of this definition are notable in that, where applicable circumstances arise, they would require a designated person to determine whether a particular person may be equivalent to a spouse (or the spouse of a child) under the laws of a foreign jurisdiction. Section 37(11) makes provision as regards when the Minister for Justice and Law Reform may prescribe a class of family member of a politically exposed person for the purposes of part (g) of this definition.

"specified official"
There will of course be Irish persons who come within some of the categories of official mentioned and who could well be considered, as s.37(1) requires, to reside in a place outside Ireland. So, for example,

Irish MEPs may come within category (b), Irish members of the European Court of Justice and the European Court of Human Rights may come within category (c), Irish members of the European Court of Auditors may come within category (d), and Irish ambassadors and chargés d'affairs and high-ranking military officers resident abroad may come within category (e).

Enhanced customer due diligence – correspondent banking relationships

38.—(1) A credit institution shall not enter into a correspondent banking relationship with another credit institution ("the respondent institution") situated in a place other than a Member State unless, prior to commencing the relationship, the credit institution—

(a) has gathered sufficient information about the respondent institution to understand fully the nature of the business of that institution,

(b) is satisfied on reasonable grounds, based on publicly available information, that the reputation of the respondent institution, and the quality of supervision or monitoring of the operation of that institution in the place, are sound,

(c) is satisfied on reasonable grounds, having assessed the anti-money laundering and anti-terrorist financing controls applied by the respondent institution, that those controls are sound,

(d) has ensured that approval is obtained from the senior management of the credit institution,

(e) has documented the responsibilities of each institution in applying anti-money laundering and anti-terrorist financing controls to customers in the conduct of the correspondent banking relationship and, in particular—

    (i) the responsibilities of the credit institution arising under this Part, and

    (ii) any responsibilities of the respondent institution arising under requirements equivalent to those specified in the Third Money Laundering Directive,

and

(f) in the case of a proposal that customers of the respondent institution have direct access to a payable-through account held with the credit institution in the name of the respondent institution, is satisfied on reasonable grounds that the respondent institution—

    (i) has identified and verified the identity of those customers, and is able to provide to the credit institution, upon request, the documents (whether or not in electronic form) or information used by the credit institution to identify and verify the identity, of those customers,

    (ii) has applied measures equivalent to the measure referred to in *section 35(1)* in relation to those customers, and

    (iii) is applying measures equivalent to the measure referred to in *section 35(3)* in relation to those customers.

(2) A credit institution that fails to comply with this section commits an offence and is liable—

(*a*) on summary conviction, to a fine not exceeding €5,000 or imprisonment for a term not exceeding 12 months (or both), or

(*b*) on conviction on indictment, to a fine or imprisonment for a term not exceeding 5 years (or both).

Section Note

Under s.38 of the Act, which largely accords with the seventh of the FATF 40 Recommendations (see FATF, *FATF 40 Recommendations*, p. 6), a credit institution in Ireland must not (as correspondent bank) enter into a banking relationship with another credit institution (the respondent bank) situate in a place other than a Member State unless the correspondent credit institution has undertaken the steps prescribed in s.38(1). One slight deviation between s.38 and the seventh of the FATF 40 Recommendations is that the recommendation is intended to apply to "cross-border correspondent banking and other similar relationships" whereas s.38 (and Art.13(3) of the Directive, which s.38 implements) apply to certain cross border correspondent banking relationships only.

Section 38(1)(f) of the Act refers to a "payable-through account". The term is not defined in the Act (or in Art.13(3)(e) of the Directive, the provision that s.38(1)(f) transposes into Irish law). However the term "Payable-through accounts" is defined in the Glossary to the FATF 40 Recommendations as referring to "correspondent accounts that are used directly by third parties to transact business on their own behalf" (FATF, *FATF 40 Recommendations*, p.17). As the term "payable-through accounts" is used in the seventh of the FATF 40 Recommendations and as that recommendation informs Art.13(3)(e) of the Directive and hence s.38(1)(f) of the Act, the definition of the term in the Glossary to the FATF 40 Recommendations is of note.

Under s.38(2) failure by a credit institution to comply with s.38 is a criminal offence. On offences generally under the Act, see the table of offences arising under the Act (and the penalties for same) in Appendix 2 of this text.

Designated person's discretion to apply additional enhanced customer due diligence measures

39.—(1) Nothing in this Chapter prevents a designated person from applying measures in relation to a customer or beneficial owner that are additional to those specified in this Chapter, for the purposes of preventing or detecting money laundering or terrorist financing.

(2) Without prejudice to the circumstances in which a designated person may apply such additional measures, the designated person may do so

when the designated person considers that there is a heightened risk of money laundering or terrorist financing.

Section Note

Section 39 makes clear that nothing in Ch.3 of Pt.4 prevents a designated person from applying CDD measures additional to those specified in Ch.3, in particular where a designated person considers that there is a heightened risk of money laundering or terrorist financing. Offhand it is perhaps open to question whether a designated person would seek lightly to impose CDD requirements very different from those identified in any guidelines approved under s.107 of the Act, not least because to do so could place that designated person at a potential competitive disadvantage if availing of its products and services acquired the reputation of involving a degree of bureaucracy not known at rival designated persons subject to the same legal and regulatory obligations. Of course any designated person who/ which had regard to such commercial considerations when determining the scope of its legal obligations would perhaps be treading dangerous ground given the relative ease with which a criminal offence arises under Ch.3.

Reliance on other persons to carry out customer due diligence

40.—(1) In this section, "relevant third party" means—

(*a*) a person, carrying on business as a designated person in the State—
  (i) that is a credit institution,
  (ii) that is a financial institution (other than an undertaking that is a financial institution solely because the undertaking provides either foreign exchange services or payment services, or both),
  (iii) who is an external accountant or auditor and who is also a member of a designated accountancy body,
  (iv) who is a tax adviser, and who is also a solicitor or a member of a designated accountancy body or of the Irish Taxation Institute,
  (v) who is a relevant independent legal professional, or
  (vi) who is a trust or company service provider, and who is also a member of a designated accountancy body, a solicitor or authorised to carry on business by the Central Bank and Financial Services Authority of Ireland,

(*b*) a person carrying on business in another Member State who is supervised or monitored for compliance with the requirements specified in the Third Money Laundering Directive, in accordance with Section 2 of Chapter V of that Directive, and is—
  (i) a credit institution authorised to operate as a credit institution under the laws of the Member State,
  (ii) a financial institution (other than an undertaking that is a financial institution solely because the undertaking provides either foreign exchange services or payment services, or both) and authorised to

operate as a financial institution under the laws of the Member State, or

(iii) an external accountant, auditor, tax adviser, legal professional or trust or company service provider subject to mandatory professional registration or mandatory professional supervision under the laws of the other Member State,

or

(c) a person who carries on business in a place designated under *section 31*, is supervised or monitored in the place for compliance with requirements equivalent to those specified in the Third Money Laundering Directive, and is—

(i) a credit institution authorised to operate as a credit institution under the laws of the place,

(ii) a financial institution (other than an undertaking that is a financial institution solely because the undertaking provides either foreign exchange services or payment services, or both) authorised to operate as a financial institution under the laws of the place, or

(iii) an external accountant, auditor, tax adviser, legal professional or trust or company service provider subject to mandatory professional registration or mandatory professional supervision under the laws of the place.

(2) A reference in *subsection (1)(b)(iii)* and *(c)(iii)* to a legal professional is a reference to a person who, by way of business, provides legal or notarial services.

(3) Subject to *subsections (4)* and *(5)*, a designated person may rely on a relevant third party to apply, in relation to a customer of the designated person, any of the measures that the designated person is required to apply, in relation to the customer, under *section 33* or *35(1)*.

(4) A designated person may rely on a relevant third party to apply a measure under *section 33* or *35(1)* only if—

(a) there is an arrangement between the designated person (or, in the case of a designated person who is an employee, the designated person's employer) and the relevant third party under which it has been agreed that the designated person may rely on the relevant third party to apply any such measure, and

(b) the designated person is satisfied, on the basis of the arrangement, that the relevant third party will forward to the designated person, as soon as practicable after a request from the designated person, any documents (whether or not in electronic form) or information relating to the customer that has been obtained by the relevant third party in applying the measure.

(5) A designated person who relies on a relevant third party to apply a measure under *section 33* or *35(1)* remains liable, under *section 33* or *35(1)*, for any failure to apply the measure.

(6) A reference in this section to a relevant third party on whom a designated person may rely to apply a measure under *section 33* or *35(1)* does not include a reference to a person who applies the measure as an outsourcing service provider or an agent of the designated person.

(7) Nothing in this section prevents a designated person applying a measure under *section 33* or *35(1)* by means of an outsourcing service provider or agent provided that the designated person remains liable for any failure to apply the measure.

Section Note

Recital (27) to the Directive states that "In order to avoid repeated customer identification procedures, leading to delays and inefficiency in business, it is appropriate, subject to suitable safeguards, to allow customers to be introduced whose identification has been carried out elsewhere. Where an institution or person covered by this Directive relies on a third party, the ultimate responsibility for the customer due diligence procedure remains with the institution or person to whom the customer is introduced." Section 40 commences with a lengthy definition of who constitutes a "relevant third party". Section 40(3), though it does not refer to an introduction arrangement, would facilitate such a process, providing that, subject to certain conditions identified in s.40(4) and (5), a designated person may rely on a relevant third party to apply such CDD measures in respect of a customer as are required to be applied by that designated person in relation to such customer under s.33 or 35(1) of the Act. A good example of where this might occur would be between a credit institution and another financial institution (of a class referred to in s.40(1)(a)(ii)) within the same group of companies where a customer is introduced by one to the other. The reference in s.40(1)(a)(vi) has now been amended to refer to the Central Bank of Ireland. (Per the Central Bank Reform Act 2010 (No. 23 of 2010), s.15(14) and Schedule 2, Pt.14). S.40(4) makes provision as regards the agreement that is to be established between the designated person (or the designated person's employer, if appropriate) and such "relevant third party". Section 40(5) makes clear that in the case of reliance on such relevant third party it is the designated person that remains liable for any breach of s.33 or 35(1). As failure by a designated person to comply with these provisions is a criminal offence, it is perhaps open to any question whether any prudent designated person should rely on a relevant third party in the manner anticipated by s.40. Section 40(7) makes clear that nothing in s.40 prevents a designated person from relying on an outsourcing service provider or agent to apply CDD measures under s.33 or 35(1) provided the designated person remains liable for any failure to apply the measure. Again, the overriding question that arises in this context is whether any prudent designated person should involve a third party in the performance of functions for which ultimately the designated person remains responsible. The wording of s.40(7) is of interest in that it suggests that a designated person could perhaps have outsourced liability for compliance with s.33 and/or 35(1) but for this provision.

CHAPTER 4

Reporting of suspicious transactions and of transactions involving certain places

General Note

Ch.4 imposes a variety of reporting obligations on a "designated person", which term enjoys an expanded meaning in Ch.4 (by virtue of s.41). The key elements of Ch.4 are summarised hereafter. Section 42 requires a designated person – where the designated person knows, suspects or has reasonable grounds to suspect on the basis of information obtained in the course of carrying on business as a designated person (not otherwise) that another person has been (or is) engaged in an offence of money laundering or terrorist financing – to report that knowledge, suspicion or reasonable grounds to the Garda Síochána and the Revenue Commissioners, *i.e.* the obligation is not to report another person as such, though a report will typically involve a reference to one or more particular persons (*cf.* s.42(6)(b) in this regard). Save as provided in s.46, failure to comply with of s.42 is an offence. Section 43 requires a designated person to report to the Garda Síochána and the Revenue Commissioners any service that such designated person provides or carries out in the course of carrying on business as a designated person and which is connected with a place designated under s.32 of the Act. Failure to comply with s.43 is an offence. Section 44 allows for reports made under s.43 or 44 to be routed in the first instance through an internal reporting process within an employer and makes it a defence for a person charged with an offence under s.42 or 43 to prove that such person was at the relevant time an employee who availed of such an internal reporting process. Section 45 allows reported information to be used in the investigation of any offence. Section 46 limits the circumstances in which disclosure of information is required. Section 47 provides that disclosure in accordance with Ch.4 shall not be treated as a breach of any restriction on disclosure imposed by any other enactment (*i.e.* other than the Act) or rule of law on the person making the disclosure (or by any person on whose behalf such disclosure is made). Neither Ch.4 nor any other provision of the Act seeks to implement the reporting process which the nineteenth of the FATF 40 Recommendations (FATF, *FATF 40 Recommendations*, p.9) recommends that countries should consider, whereby "banks and other financial institutions and intermediaries would report all domestic and international currency transactions above a fixed amount, to a national central agency with a computerised data base, available to competent authorities for use in money laundering or terrorist financing cases, subject to strict safeguards to ensure proper use of the information". Diagram 4 summarises the provisions of ss.41 to 47.

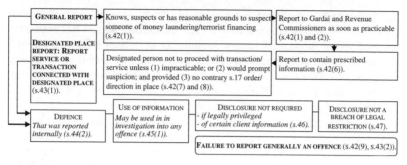

Diagram 4.

Interpretation (*Chapter 4*)

41.—In this Chapter, a reference to a designated person includes a reference to any person acting, or purporting to act, on behalf of the designated person, including any agent, employee, partner, director or other officer of, or any person engaged under a contract for services with, the designated person.

Section Note

Section 41 expands the definition of "designated person" established in s.25 to include any person acting or purporting to act on behalf of the designated person, including certain named categories of person. The effect of s.41 is to extend the reporting obligations established by Ch.4 to an array of persons who would not otherwise be caught by its provisions.

Requirement for designated persons and related persons to report suspicious transactions

42.—(1) A designated person who knows, suspects or has reasonable grounds to suspect, on the basis of information obtained in the course of carrying on business as a designated person, that another person has been or is engaged in an offence of money laundering or terrorist financing shall report to the Garda Síochána and the Revenue Commissioners that knowledge or suspicion or those reasonable grounds.

(2) The designated person shall make the report as soon as practicable after acquiring that knowledge or forming that suspicion, or acquiring those reasonable grounds to suspect, that the other person has been or is engaged in money laundering or terrorist financing.

(3) For the purposes of *subsections (1)* and *(2)*, a designated person is taken not to have reasonable grounds to know or suspect that another person commits an offence on the basis of having received information until the person has scrutinised the information in the course of reasonable business practice (including automated banking transactions).

(4) For the purposes of *subsections (1)* and *(2)*, a designated person may have reasonable grounds to suspect that another person has been or is engaged in an offence of money laundering or terrorist financing if the designated person is unable to apply any measures specified in *section 33(2)* or *(4)*, *35(1)* or *37(1)*, *(3)*, *(4)* or *(6)*, in relation to a customer, as a result of any failure on the part of the customer to provide the designated person with documents or information.

(5) Nothing in *subsection (4)* limits the circumstances in which a designated person may have reasonable grounds, on the basis of information obtained in the course of carrying out business as a designated person, to suspect that another person has committed an offence of money laundering or terrorist financing.

(6) A designated person who is required to report under this section shall disclose the following information in the report:

(*a*) the information on which the designated person's knowledge, suspicion or reasonable grounds are based;

(*b*) the identity, if the designated person knows it, of the person who the designated person knows, suspects or has reasonable grounds to suspect has been or is engaged in an offence of money laundering or terrorist financing;

(*c*) the whereabouts, if the designated person knows them, of the property the subject of the money laundering, or the funds the subject of the terrorist financing, as the case may be;

(*d*) any other relevant information.

(7) A designated person who is required to make a report under this section shall not proceed with any suspicious transaction or service connected with the report, or with a transaction or service the subject of the report, prior to the sending of the report to the Garda Síochána and the Revenue Commissioners unless—

(*a*) it is not practicable to delay or stop the transaction or service from proceeding, or

(*b*) the designated person is of the reasonable opinion that failure to proceed with the transaction or service may result in the other person suspecting that a report may be (or may have been) made or that an investigation may be commenced or in the course of being conducted.

(8) Nothing in *subsection (7)* authorises a designated person to proceed with a service or transaction if the person has been directed or ordered not to proceed with the service or transaction under *section 17* and the direction or order is in force.

(9) Except as provided by *section 46*, a person who fails to comply with this section commits an offence and is liable—

(*a*) on summary conviction, to a fine not exceeding €5,000 or imprisonment for a term not exceeding 12 months (or both), or

(*b*) on conviction on indictment, to a fine or imprisonment for a term not exceeding 5 years (or both).

(10) A reference in *subsection (7)* to a suspicious transaction or service is a reference to a transaction or service that there are reasonablegrounds for suspecting would, if it were to proceed—

(*a*) comprise money laundering or terrorist financing, or
(*b*) assist in money laundering or terrorist financing.

Section Note

Section 42(1) establishes a reporting obligation for a designated person (as that term is defined in ss. 29 and 41). The most natural reading of s.42(1) would seem to be that information to which it refers as having been "obtained" must have been obtained by the reporting designated person in the course of its carrying on business as a designated person, though the provision could perhaps have been clearer in this regard. (See further in this regard the consideration of s.49(1) and (2) below).

Knowledge, suspicion or "reasonable grounds" to suspect that another person has been (or is) engaged in an offence of money laundering or terrorist financing each suffice to give rise to a reporting obligation. There is abundant case-law on what constitutes a suspicion but the recent decision of the English Court of Appeal in *R. v Da Silva* [2006] 4 All ER 900, perhaps summarises matters best when (at 906) it describes suspicion as involving a defendant thinking that "there is a possibility, which is more than fanciful, that the relevant facts exist. A vague feeling of unease would not suffice". So just because a matter gives cause for pause would necessarily not mean that a suspicion arises, though it ought perhaps to prompt further enquiry. The Act does not indicate what the consequences are for a designated person where ostensibly "reasonable grounds" turn out not to have been reasonable at all: it is at least arguable that a disclosure of information in such circumstances was never in accordance with Ch.4 of Pt.4 and thus that the immunity arising under s.47 of the Act does not apply.

Section 42(1) was the subject of a proposed amendment in the Seanad that would have seen the reporting obligation reduced to an obligation to report to the Garda Síochána only. Per Senator Ivana Bacik, who moved the relevant proposed amendment:

> "I must point out again that I am not seeking to water down the Bill. I fully support the need for reporting requirements and the objectives of section 42, but I simply wish to ensure we avoid bureaucratic overload for those seeking to act in full compliance with the legislation. Should it not be sufficient to contact the Garda with such information, knowing it will pass it on, if necessary, to the Revenue Commissioners? In addition, there is the possibility, when reports are sent to two agencies, that a report might fall

> between two stools, with each agency thinking the other is doing something about it. It does seem there is an issue with regard to reporting. It may be that dual reporting is required under the directive although, I must say, I have not looked." (201(9) *Díospóireachtaí Parlaiminte* (Seanad Éireann) (11.3.10), p.593).

The relevant provisions of the Directive are contained in Ch.III of same. Consistent with the thirteenth of the FATF 40 Recommendations (FATF, *FATF 40 Recommendations*, p.8), Ch.III anticipates that a single report would be made to a national "financial intelligence unit" (or "FIU") which serves as a national centre for "receiving, analysing and disseminating to the competent authorities, disclosures of information which concern potential money laundering, potential terrorist financing or are required by national legislation or regulation". (Directive, Art.21). (The establishment of such an FIU is recommended in the twenty-sixth of the FATF 40 Recommendations (FATF, *FATF 40 Recommendations*, p.10)). Thus Ch.III does not require, let alone anticipate, though neither does it prohibit, a dual reporting structure. In Ireland, the Garda Bureau of Fraud Investigation has, since 1995, hosted Ireland's FIU. It receives suspicious transaction reports made to the Garda Síochána and disseminates them to financial investigation units within the Garda for further investigation. The making of reports to the Revenue Commissioners (in practice, the Suspicious Transactions Reports Office of the Revenue Commissioners) operates in tandem with the making of reports to the Garda Síochána (in practice, the Garda Bureau of Fraud Investigation).

The reply of the Minister for Justice, Equality and Law Reform to Senator Bacik's proposed amendment affords an insight on the thinking of the Garda Síochána and the Revenue Commissioners regarding the dual reporting structure under Ireland's anti-money laundering and terrorist financing regime and the success of that dual reporting structure to this time. Per the Minister:

> "Both the Garda and the Revenue Commissioners, in the context of this legislation, feel it is important that there be an obligation to report to both of them. The suggestion that reports might fall between two stools is not realistic because of the fairly good connection between the Revenue Commissioners and the Garda in such areas. They already work on a multi-agency basis in this regard....Under existing provisions of the Criminal Justice Act 1994 with regard to the reporting of suspicious transactions, designated persons are obliged to report both to the Garda and to the Revenue Commissioners. Section 42 does not in fact change this obligation. The system has worked perfectly well. The reporting requirements to the Revenue Commissioners have proved a significant tool in combating tax evasion. I understand that about €40 million in additional taxes has been recovered in cases in which the information in a suspicious transaction report has been significant in bringing a case to the attention of the authorities or to a conclusion. Such reports have also assisted in a

number of criminal prosecutions." (201(9) *Díospóireachtaí Parlaiminte* (Seanad Éireann) (11.3.10), p.594).

What the reply suggests is that, as well as being a useful tool in combating money laundering and terrorist financing, the anti-money laundering and anti-terrorist financing legislation has been useful for the Revenue Commissioners in identifying tax evasion. This last dimension of the anti-money laundering and anti-terrorist financing legislation seems otherwise somewhat underplayed by the authorities, not least in the choice of name for the Act which refers to money laundering and terrorist financing but not tax evasion.

Section 42(2) is concerned with the timing of reports made under s.42(1). They must be made "as soon as practicable" after acquiring the knowledge, forming the suspicion or acquiring the 'reasonable grounds to suspect' that is or are the basis of the report. This is a rigorous standard and does not allow for much delay from acquiring the knowledge, forming the suspicion or acquiring the 'reasonable grounds to suspect' to the making of a report.

Section 42(3) in effect acknowledges the practical reality that a designated person may be in possession of information but not yet have any real cognisance of that information. The classic example of this is where a corporate entity has electronic systems data available to it but no-one within that entity has yet scrutinised that information. However, s.42(3) does not give a *carte blanche* to designated persons in this regard. Thus it provides that a designated person is taken not to have reasonable grounds to know or suspect that another commits an offence on the basis of information received until the person has scrutinised that information "in the course of reasonable business practice".

Section 42(4) makes clear that where the failure of a customer to provide a designated person with documents or information has the result that such designated person is unable to apply any measures specified in the named provisions, this in and of itself may constitute reasonable grounds to suspect another person of an offence of money laundering or terrorist financing (and thus, for example, justify the making of a report under s.42(1)), though of course it is possible that the customer failure may have an entirely innocent cause. Section 42(5) makes clear that s.42(4) is meant by way of clarification and not limitation on the circumstances in which a designated person may have reasonable grounds to suspect another of money laundering or terrorist financing.

Section 42(6) identifies the information to be contained in a s.42 report.

A key question that arises for a designated person is what to do as regards dealings with or connected with a person in respect of whom a s.42 report falls to be made. Section 42(7) provides that such a designated person must not, prior to the sending of the relevant report to the Garda Síochána and the Revenue Commissioners, proceed with any "suspicious transaction or service" connected with such report (the quoted term is defined in s.42(10)), or with a transaction or service the subject of such report unless one of two sets of circumstances pertains. These are identified in s.42(7)(a) and (b). These provisions present a potential difficulty for designated persons as it is they who must decide whether it is "not practicable" to delay/stop a transaction or service, and it is they who must be of the "reasonable opinion" that failure to proceed may result in any of the difficulties identified in s.42(7)(b), and it is they who must suffer the consequences if it is later determined that it was practicable to delay/stop a transaction or service or that the opinion of which they were apparently possessed was not reasonable. In practice, a telephone call to the Garda Bureau of Fraud Investigation, where feasible, may help to resolve some of the potential practical difficulties arising. S.42(7) also of course presents a potential difficulty vis-à-vis s.17 of the Act (considered above) in that it would appear to allow a designated person to proceed with a particular service or transaction notwithstanding that the designated person has been ordered under s.17 not to so proceed and the applicable s.17 order or direction is in force; s.42(8) makes clear that this is not so and that a s.17 order or direction that is in force takes precedence in this regard. The derogation established by s.42(7) is consistent with recital (30) of the Directive, though the recital does note that such derogation "should be without prejudice to the international obligations accepted by the Member States to freeze without delay funds or other assets of terrorists, terrorist organisations or those who finance terrorism, in accordance with the relevant United Nations Security Council resolutions". Except as provided by s.46 (considered below), failure by a person to comply with s.42 is a criminal offence (per s.42(9)). On offences generally under the Act, see the table of offences arising under the Act (and the penalties for same) in Appendix 2 of this text.

Requirement for designated persons to report transactions connected with places designated under *section 32*

43.—(1) A designated person shall report to the Garda Síochána and Revenue Commissioners any service or transaction, that—

(a) the designated person provides or carries out in the course of carrying on business as a designated person, and

(b) is connected with a place that is designated under *section 32*.

(2) A person who fails to comply with this section commits an offence and is liable—

(a) on summary conviction, to a fine not exceeding €5,000 or imprisonment for a term not exceeding 12 months (or both), or

(b) on conviction on indictment, to a fine or imprisonment for a term not exceeding 5 years (or both).

Section Note

In the Bill, as introduced, there was, in s.43, an obligation to report to the Garda Síochána only; the Revenue Commissioners were added later by way of Government amendment. Failure by a person to comply with s.43 is (per s.43(2)) a criminal offence. On offences generally under the Act, see the table of offences arising under the Act (and the penalties for same) in Appendix 2 of this text.

Defence – internal reporting procedures

44.—(1) Without prejudice to the way in which a report may be made under *section 42* or *43*, such a report may be made in accordance with an internal reporting procedure established by an employer for the purpose of facilitating the operation of the section concerned.

(2) It is a defence for a person charged with an offence under *section 42* or *43* to prove that the person was, at the time of the purported offence, an employee who made a report under that section, in accordance with such an internal reporting procedure, to another person.

Section Note

Section 44 allows for reports made under s.43 or 44 to be routed in the first instance through an internal reporting process within an employer and makes it a defence for a person charged with an offence under s.42 or 43 to prove that such person was at the time of the purported offence an employee who availed of such an internal reporting process. Typically such an internal reporting process will involve the making of suspicious transaction reports to a senior staff member known as the "Money Laundering Reporting Officer" (or "MLRO") who will decide which of these internal reports justifies the making of a report to the Garda Síochána and the Revenue Commissioners by and for the employer. There is no requirement in the legislation that employers who are designated persons must appoint a money laundering reporting officer but such a step is perhaps prudent, not least in facilitating the streamlined provision of information to the designated person so that it itself can comply with its reporting obligations under the Act. Clearly any designated person that operates such an internal reporting process will want to ensure that it is sufficiently efficient as not to place the designated person in breach of its obligation under s.42(2) to make a report "as soon as practicable" after acquiring the knowledge or forming the suspicion or acquiring the reasonable grounds to suspect that give rise to a reporting obligation under s.42(1).

Use of reported and other information in investigations

45.—(1) Information included in a report under this Chapter may be used in an investigation into money laundering or terrorist financing or any other offence.

(2) Nothing in this section limits the information that may be used in an investigation into any offence.

Section Note

Although a similar provision existed under the previously extant anti-money laundering and anti-terrorist financing regime (s.57(1A) of the Criminal Justice Act 1994) and although the provision makes good sense, it may nonetheless be a surprise to some that a report made under Ch.4 may be used in the investigation of any offence. By stating that information in a report made under Ch.4 may be used in the investigation into money laundering, terrorist financing or any other offence, it would perhaps be possible to conclude that no other information may be used in the investigation of any such offence: s.45(2) makes clear that such a reading is wrong and that nothing in s.45 limits the information that may be used in an investigation into any offence. The reply of the Minister quoted in the context of section 42 above suggests that one use of such information as is referred to in s.45(1) will be to investigate tax evasion.

Disclosure not required in certain circumstances

46.—(1) Nothing in this Chapter requires the disclosure of information that is subject to legal privilege.

(2) Nothing in this Chapter requires a relevant professional adviser to disclose information that he or she has received from or obtained in relation to a client in the course of ascertaining the legal position of the client.

(3) *Subsection (2)* does not apply to information received from or obtained in relation to a client with the intention of furthering a criminal purpose.

Section Note

The reporting obligation established by s.42 clearly presents a difficulty in that in and of itself it could require (a) a person to disclose information that is subject to legal privilege or (b) a relevant professional adviser to disclose information obtained by that adviser from a client in the course of ascertaining the legal position of a client. Section 46 makes clear that this is not so. The rationale for the provision seems clear: there is a significant public policy interest in ensuring that legally privileged documentation remains privileged and also in ensuring that there is full and frank disclosure between clients and advisors when an advisor is seeking to ascertain a client's legal position.

The guidance given by the Law Society of Ireland to its members as regards s.46(1) is of particular interest in that it makes clear how, because the disclosure of legally privileged information is not required by Ch.4 of Pt.4, the professional obligations of solicitors vis-à-vis their clients has the effect that they are in fact required *not* to make a report where the s.46(1) exemption may be invoked. Per the Law Society:

> "If a professional adviser considers that the information or other matter on which his knowledge or suspicion is based came to him in privileged circumstances, he is obliged to apply the reporting **exemption** and so has no discretion to make a money laundering report. In such circumstances, he should consider whether he should continue to act....Nothing requires the disclosure of information that is subject to legal privilege. This means that communications between a legal adviser and client are not to be disclosed without the consent of the client....Whether or not the reporting exemption applies needs to be considered carefully....If in doubt, it is recommended that a solicitor would seek independent advice." (Law Society of Ireland, *Guidance Notes for Solicitors on Anti-Money Laundering Obligations* (Dublin: 2006), p.59 *et seq.*).

Section 46(2) makes provision as regards information received from a client by a "relevant professional adviser" (*i.e.* an accountant, auditor or tax advisor who is a member of a designated accountancy body or of the Irish Taxation Institute (per s.24(1)), or obtained in relation to a client, "in the course of ascertaining the legal position of the client", indicating that nothing in Ch.4 of Pt.4 requires the disclosure of such information. This is consistent with recital (21) to the Directive which provides that:

> "[I]n the case of auditors, external accountants and tax advisors, who, in some Member States, may defend or represent a client in the context of judicial proceedings or ascertain a client's legal position, the information they obtain in the performance of those risks should not be subject to the reporting obligations in accordance with this Directive."

The wording of s.46(2) suggests that (subject to s.46(3)) there is no obligation on a relevant professional adviser to disclose any information received or obtained in the manner described, provided it was received/obtained "in the course of ascertaining the legal position of the client", even if the information so received/obtained does not pertain to the matter in respect of which the legal position of the client is being ascertained. So, for example, a throwaway comment by a client regarding a matter in respect of which the client's legal position did not fall to be ascertained would appear to come within the exemption arising under s.46(7) received by the relevant professional adviser from the client in the course of a conversation seeking to ascertain the legal position of the client.

Disclosure not to be treated as breach

47.—The disclosure of information by a person in accordance with this Chapter shall not be treated, for any purpose, as a breach of any restriction imposed by any other enactment or rule of law on disclosure by the person or any other person on whose behalf the disclosure is made.

Section Note

Section 46 is of no assistance to persons such as credit institutions which are in possession of customer information that is not subject to legal privilege, who-by virtue of the definition of "relevant professional adviser" in s.24(1) of the Act-simply cannot be acting as a relevant professional adviser vis-à-vis a customer, yet who, for example, are subject to an implied contractual duty of confidentiality and also will be subject to obligations under data protection legislation if a customer is a natural person. Section 47 of the Act, considered also in the context of s.7(7) above and s.112 below, makes it possible for a person to disclose information in accordance with Ch.4 without thereby placing that person (or any person on whose behalf such disclosure is made) in breach of a prohibition on the disclosure of such information under any other enactment (*i.e.* any enactment other than the Act) or rule of law. Though there are differences of terminology, s.47 is consistent with the fourteenth of the FATF 40 Recommendations (FATF, *FATF 40 Recommendations*, p.8) which requires that the exemption from liability be enjoyed even where the relevant "good faith" disclosure is done without knowing "precisely what the underlying criminal activity was, and regardless of whether illegal activity actually occurred". Section 47 does not have an express good faith requirement. However, s.47 does require that the disclosure of information be in accordance with Ch.4 and it is difficult to see how a person not acting in good faith could, for example, know or (genuinely) suspect someone to be or have been engaged in an offence of money laundering or terrorist financing for the purposes of s.42. It is interesting to compare the provision made in s.47 with that extant under s.57 of the Criminal Justice Act 1994 (repealed in part by s.4(1) of the Act). That earlier provision states that a disclosure of a type to which it refers "shall not be treated as a breach of any restriction upon the disclosure of information imposed by statute or otherwise and shall not involve the person or body making the disclosure (including their directors, employees and officers) in *liability of any kind.*" (Emphasis added). In a similar vein, Art.26 of the Directive provides that:

> "The disclosure in good faith as foreseen in Articles 22(1) and 23 by an institution or person covered by this Directive or by an employee or director of such an institution referred to in Articles 22 and 23 shall not constitute a breach of any restriction on disclosure of information imposed by contract or by any legislative, regulatory or administrative provision, and shall not involve the institution or person or its directors or employees in *liability of any kind*". (Emphasis added).

In the context of s.112 of the Act (considered below) questions were raised in the Dáil during the passage of the Bill through that House as to whether in effect such a form of immunity from liability ought to be granted by s.112. A similar point could perhaps have been made with regard to s.47 and would perhaps have met with the same logic that the Minster for Justice, Equality and Law Reform employed when the point was raised in the context of s.112, namely that civil or criminal liability cannot arise unless there is a breach of an enactment or rule of law. If so, of course, a question perhaps arises as to why the EU draftsman has also referred, in Art.26 of the Directive, to "liability of any kind".

CHAPTER 5

Tipping off by designated persons

General Note

In essence, tipping off involves a designated person in defined circumstances making a disclosure that is likely to prejudice a money laundering or terrorist financing investigation. Ch.5 is in some ways an unusual Chapter in that the offence of tipping off (which may be committed in two ways) is established in one section (s.49), the rest of the Chapter being largely taken up with establishing various defences to this offence. There are nine such defences: (1) where a defendant discloses only certain details regarding a s.17 direction/order to a customer of either the defendant or the designated person for whom the defendant makes the disclosure (s.50); (2) where, in effect, a staff member or like individual within an undertaking makes a disclosure to another such staff member or individual (s.51(1)); (3) where there is an intra-group disclosure by or for a credit/financial institution to a credit/financial institution, provided the latter institution is situate in an EU member state (or a place designated under section 31) (s.51(2)); (4) where there is a disclosure between certain professionals acting within entities with common ownership, management or control and both the discloser and the recipient of the disclosure carry on business in an EU member state (or a place designated under section 31) (s.51(3)); (5) where the disclosure is by or for a credit institution/financial institution/legal adviser/relevant professional adviser of a particular kind to a like person or entity in defined circumstances (s.52); (6) where the disclosure is by a person to the competent authority with responsibility for that person or the person for whom the disclosure was made (s53(1)(a)); (7) where the disclosure is for the purpose of the detection, investigation or prosecution of an offence, whether or not in Ireland (s.53(1)(b)); (8) where the person does not know or suspect, at the time of the disclosure, that the disclosure is likely to have the effect of prejudicing an investigation into whether an offence of money laundering or terrorist financing has been committed; (s.53(1)(c)); and (9) where the disclosure occurs in a defined adviser-to-client context, is solely to the effect that the adviser will no longer provide a particular service to a client, the adviser no longer does so provide thereafter, and the adviser makes any report required in relation to the client in accordance with Chapter 4 of Part 4 of the Act (s.53(2)).

Interpretation (*Chapter 5*)

48.—In this Chapter, "legal adviser" means a barrister or solicitor.

Section Note

It will be recalled that the terms "barrister" and "solicitor" are themselves defined in s.24 as meaning respectively a practising barrister and a practising solicitor. There are of course many barristers and solicitors who are not engaged in practice.

Tipping off

49.—(1) A designated person who knows or suspects, on the basis of information obtained in the course of carrying on business as a designated person, that a report has been, or is required to be, made under *Chapter 4* shall not make any disclosure that is likely to prejudice an investigation that may be conducted following the making of the report under that Chapter.

(2) A designated person who knows or suspects, on the basis of information obtained by the person in the course of carrying on business as a designated person, that an investigation is being contemplated or is being carried out into whether an offence of money laundering or terrorist financing has been committed, shall not make any disclosure that is likely to prejudice the investigation.

(3) A person who fails to comply with this section commits an offence and is liable—

(a) on summary conviction, to a fine not exceeding €5,000 or imprisonment for a term not exceeding 12 months (or both), or
(b) on conviction on indictment, to a fine or imprisonment for a term not exceeding 5 years (or both).

(4) In this section, a reference to a designated person includes a reference to any person acting, or purporting to act, on behalf of the designated person, including any agent, employee, partner, director or other officer of, or any person engaged under a contract for services with, the designated person.

Section Note

Section 49 establishes the elements of the offence of tipping off. There are two ways in which the offence may be committed: first, a designated person who knows or suspects, on the basis of information obtained in the course of carrying on business as a designated person, that a report has been or is required to be made under Ch.4 makes a disclosure that is likely to prejudice an investigation that may be conducted following the making of such report (s.49(1)); second, a designated person knows or suspects, on the basis of information obtained by the designated person in the course of carrying on business as a designated person, that an investigation is being contemplated or carried out into whether an offence of money laundering or terrorist financing has been committed and makes a disclosure that is likely to prejudice the investigation (s.49(2)). There is English case-law that suggests that the form of the disclosure is not relevant, so for example that it could be by word, sign or deed. (See *The Bank v A Ltd.* [2000] Lloyd's Rep. Bank 271 at 278).

Section 49(2) makes clear that such information as is referred to therein must have been "obtained by the [designated] person in the course of carrying on business as a designated person." By contrast, s.49(1), which in this respect bears a close resemblance to s.42(1) (considered above), is less exact, referring to "information obtained in the course of carrying on business as a designated person." It is not clear that the different wordings are intended to be interpreted differently but it is clear that they can be interpreted differently,

The Law Society of Ireland, in its guidance notes for solicitors, raises a potential form of tipping off that is of interest both to solicitors and their clients. This potential form of tipping off arises where a solicitor ceases to act for a client for reasons connected with the Act. That a solicitor should cease to act for a client is the general course of action recommended by the Law Society where a solicitor makes a s.42 report and also where a solicitor suspects a client of a money laundering offence but makes no report (a real possibility for solicitors in light of s.46(1) of the Act). Clearly a client will want to know why his or her solicitor is ceasing to act and it is of course possible that a solicitor could make a disclosure in breach of s.49 in reply. Section 53 will avail a solicitor here. Moreover, in this regard the Law Society refers to a letter to the Law Society from a former Minister for Justice, Equality and Law Reform in relation to the tipping-off offence as formulated in the Criminal Justice Act 1994 that "this does not prohibit a solicitor from informing his or her client that he or she was ceasing to act for the client or, indeed, that he or she was ceasing to act for a client because he or she was unhappy with any transaction in which the client was involved". (Law Society of Ireland *Guidance Notes for Solicitors on Anti-Money Laundering Obligations* (Dublin: 2010), p.61).

Failure by a person to comply with s.49 is (per s.49(3)) a criminal offence. (On offences generally under the Act, see the table of offences arising under the Act (and the penalties for same) in Appendix 2 of this text).

The term "designated person" enjoys the same expanded meaning under s.49(4) that is given that phrase in Ch.4 (by s.41).

Defence – disclosure to customer in case of direction or order to suspend service or transaction

50.—It is a defence in any proceedings against a person ("the defendant") for an offence under *section 49*, in relation to a disclosure, for the defendant to prove that—

(*a*) the disclosure was to a person who, at the time of the disclosure, was a customer of the defendant or of a designated person on whose behalf the defendant made the disclosure,

(*b*) the defendant, or the designated person on whose behalf the defendant made the disclosure, was directed or ordered under *section 17* not to carry out any specified service or transaction in respect of the customer, and

(*c*) the disclosure was solely to the effect that the defendant, or a designated person on whose behalf the defendant made the disclosure, had been directed by a member of the Garda Síochána, or ordered by a judge of the District Court, under *section 17* not to carry out the service or transaction for the period specified in the direction or order.

Defences – disclosures within undertaking or group

51.—(1) It is a defence in any proceedings against an individual for an offence under *section 49*, in relation to a disclosure, for the individual to prove that, at the time of the disclosure—

(*a*) he or she was an agent, employee, partner, director or other officer of, or was engaged under a contract for services by, an undertaking, and

(*b*) he or she made the disclosure to an agent, employee, partner, director or other officer of, or a person engaged under a contract for services by, the same undertaking.

(2) It is a defence in any proceedings against a person for an offence under *section 49*, in relation to a disclosure, for the person to prove that, at the time of the disclosure—

(*a*) the person was a credit institution or financial institution, or made the disclosure on behalf of a credit institution or financial institution,

(*b*) the disclosure was to a credit institution or a financial institution,

(*c*) the institution to which the disclosure was made was situated in a Member State or a place designated under *section 31*, and

(*d*) both the institution making the disclosure, or on whose behalf the disclosure was made, and the institution to which it was made belonged to the same group.

(3) It is a defence in any proceedings against a person for an offence under *section 49*, in relation to a disclosure, for the person to prove that, at the time of the disclosure—

(*a*) the person was a legal adviser or relevant professional adviser,

(*b*) both the person making the disclosure and the person to whom it was made carried on business in a Member State or in a place designated under *section 31*, and

(*c*) those persons performed their professional activities within different undertakings that shared common ownership, management or control.

Defences – other disclosures between institutions or professionals

52.—(1) This section applies to a disclosure—

(*a*) by or on behalf of a credit institution to another credit institution,

(*b*) by or on behalf of a financial institution to another financial institution,

(*c*) by or on behalf of a legal adviser to another legal adviser, or

(*d*) by or on behalf of a relevant professional adviser of a particular kind to another relevant professional adviser of the same kind.

(2) It is a defence in any proceedings against a person for an offence under *section 49*, in relation to a disclosure to which this section applies, for the person to prove that, at the time of the disclosure—

(*a*) the disclosure related to—

(i) a customer or former customer of the person (or an institution or adviser on whose behalf the person made the disclosure) and the institution or adviser to which or whom it was made, or

(ii) a transaction, or the provision of a service, involving both the person (or an institution or adviser on whose behalf the person made the disclosure) and the institution or adviser to which or whom it was made,

(*b*) the disclosure was only for the purpose of preventing money laundering or terrorist financing,

(*c*) the institution or adviser to which or whom the disclosure was made was situated in a Member State or in a place designated under *section 31*, and

(*d*) the institution or adviser making the disclosure, or on whose behalf the disclosure was made, and the institution or adviser to which or whom it was made were subject to equivalent duties of professional confidentiality and the protection of personal data (within the meaning of the Data Protection Acts 1988 and 2003).

(3) A reference in this section to a customer of an adviser includes, in the case of an adviser who is a barrister, a reference to a person who is a client of a solicitor who has sought advice from the barrister for or on behalf of the client.

Defences – other disclosures

53.—(1) It is a defence in any proceedings against a person for an offence under *section 49*, in relation to a disclosure, for the person to prove that—

(*a*) the disclosure was to the authority that, at the time of the disclosure, was the competent authority responsible for monitoring that person, or for monitoring the person on whose behalf the disclosure was made, under this Part,

(*b*) the disclosure was for the purpose of the detection, investigation or prosecution of an offence (whether or not in the State), or

(*c*) the person did not know or suspect, at the time of the disclosure, that the disclosure was likely to have the effect of prejudicing an investigation into whether an offence of money laundering or terrorist financing had been committed.

(2) It is a defence in any proceedings against a person for an offence under *section 49*, in relation to a disclosure, for the person to prove that—

(*a*) at the time of the disclosure, the person was a legal adviser or relevant professional adviser,

(*b*) the disclosure was to the person's client and solely to the effect that the person would no longer provide the particular service concerned to the client,

(*c*) the person no longer provided the particular service after so informing the client, and

(*d*) the person made any report required in relation to the client in accordance with *Chapter 4*.

CHAPTER 6

Internal policies and procedures, training and record keeping

General Note
Chapter 6 is relatively brief. It requires that a designated person adopt policies and procedures in relation to its business to prevent and detect the commission of money laundering and terrorist financing and it makes provision as regards the keeping of records by designated persons.

Internal policies and procedures and training

54.—(1) A designated person shall adopt policies and procedures, in relation to the designated person's business, to prevent and detect the commission of money laundering and terrorist financing.

(2) In particular, a designated person shall adopt policies and procedures to be followed by persons involved in the conduct of the designated person's business, that specify the designated person's obligations under this Part, including—

(*a*) the assessment and management of risks of money laundering or terrorist financing, and

(*b*) internal controls, including internal reporting procedures for the purposes of *Chapter 4*.

(3) The policies and procedures referred to in *subsection (2)* include policies and procedures dealing with—

(*a*) the identification and scrutiny of complex or large transactions, unusual patterns of transactions that have no apparent economic or visible lawful purpose and any other activity that the designated person has reasonable grounds to regard as particularly likely, by its nature, to be related to money laundering or terrorist financing, and

(*b*) measures to be taken to prevent the use for money laundering or terrorist financing of transactions or products that could favour or facilitate anonymity.

(4) The designated person shall also adopt policies and procedures in relation to the monitoring and management of compliance with, and the internal communication of, the policies and procedures referred to in *subsection (2)*.

(5) In preparing policies and procedures under this section, the designated person shall have regard to any relevant guidelines applying in relation to the designated person that have been approved under *section 107*.

(6) A designated person shall ensure that persons involved in the conduct of the designated person's business are—

(*a*) instructed on the law relating to money laundering and terrorist financing, and

(*b*) provided with ongoing training on identifying a transaction or other activity that may be related to money laundering or terrorist financing, and on how to proceed once such a transaction or activity is identified.

(7) A reference in this section to persons involved in the conduct of a designated person's business includes a reference to directors and other officers, and employees, of the designated person.

(8) A designated person who fails to comply with this section commits an offence and is liable—

(*a*) on summary conviction, to a fine not exceeding €5,000 or imprisonment for a term not exceeding 12 months (or both), or

(*b*) on conviction on indictment, to a fine or imprisonment for a term not exceeding 5 years (or both).

(9) The obligations imposed on a designated person under this section do not apply to a designated person who is an employee of another designated person.

(10) *Subsection (6)* does not apply to a designated person who is an individual and carries on business alone as a designated person.

Section Note
Section 54 of the Act accords with the fifteenth of the FATF 40 Recommendations (FATF, *FATF 40 Recommendations*, p.8). It

imposes essentially three requirements on designated persons (other than, per s.54(9), a designated person who is an employee of another designated person): first, that a designated person adopt policies and procedures, in relation to that designated person's business, including such policies and procedures as are referred to in s.54(1) to (4); second, that in preparing such policies and procedures a designated person have regard to any relevant guidelines approved under s.107 of the Act and applicable in relation to such designated person (s.54(5)); and third, that a designated person (other than a designated person who is an "individual" (a natural person) and who carries on business alone as a designated person (per s.54(10)) ensure that persons involved in the conduct of such designated person's business are (a) instructed on the law relating to money laundering and terrorist financing and (b) provided with ongoing training on (i) identifying money laundering/terrorist financing-related transactions or other activities and (ii) how to proceed once such a transaction or activity is identified (s.54(6) and (7)). Section 54(7) indicates that a reference in section 54 to "persons involved in the conduct of a designated person's business" includes directors and other officers and employees of the designated person. This provision is so wide as to effectively require that policies and procedures be established for all staff. Failure by a designated person to comply with s.54 is a criminal offence (per s.54(8)). (On offences generally under the Act, see the table of offences arising under the Act (and the penalties for same) in Appendix 2 of this text).

Keeping of records by designated persons

55.—(1) A designated person shall keep records evidencing the procedures applied, and information obtained, by the designated person
under *Chapter 3* in relation to—

(a) each customer, and

(b) in the case of a designated person to whom *section 38* applies, each correspondent banking relationship.

(2) Without prejudice to the generality of *subsection (1)*, a designated person shall take the original or a copy of all documents used by the designated person for the purposes of *Chapter 3*, including all documents used to verify the identity of customers or beneficial owners in accordance with *section 33*.

(3) A designated person shall keep records evidencing the history of services and transactions carried out in relation to each customer of the designated person.

(4) The documents and other records referred to in *subsections (1)* to *(3)* shall be retained by the designated person, at an office or other premises in the State, for a period of not less than 5 years after—

(*a*) in the case of a record referred to in *subsection (1)(a)*, the date on which the designated person ceases to provide any service to the customer concerned or the date of the last transaction (if any) with the customer, whichever is the later,

(*b*) in the case of a record referred to in *subsection (1)(b)*, the date on which the correspondent banking relationship concerned ends,

(*c*) in the case of a record referred to in *subsection (3)* evidencing the carrying out of a particular transaction by the designated person with, for or on behalf of the customer (other than a record to which *paragraph (d)* applies), the date on which the particular transaction is completed or discontinued,

(*d*) in the case of a record referred to in *subsection (3)* evidencing the carrying out of a particular occasional transaction comprised of a series of transactions, with, for or on behalf of a customer, the date on which the series of transactions is completed or discontinued, or

(*e*) in the case of a record referred to in *subsection (3)* evidencing the carrying out of a particular service for or on behalf of the customer (other than a record to which *paragraph (c)* or *(d)* applies), the date on which the particular service is completed or discontinued.

(5) *Subsection (4)(a)* extends to any record that was required to be retained under section 32(9)(*a*) of the Act of 1994 immediately before the repeal of that provision by this Act.

(6) *Subsection (4)(c)* to *(e)* extends to any record that was required to be retained under section 32(9)(*b*) of the Criminal Justice Act 1994 immediately before the repeal of that provision by this Act and for that purpose—

(*a*) a reference in *subsection (4)(c)* to *(e)* to a record referred to in *subsection (3)* includes a reference to such a record, and

(*b*) a reference in *subsection (4)(d)* to an occasional transaction comprised of a series of transactions includes a reference to a series of transactions referred to in section 32(3)(*b*) of the Criminal Justice Act 1994.

(7) A designated person may keep the records referred to in *subsections (1)* to *(6)* wholly or partly in an electronic, mechanical or other non-written form only if they are capable of being reproduced in a written form.

(8) The requirements imposed by this section are in addition to, and not in substitution for, any other requirements imposed by any other enactment or rule of law with respect to the keeping and retention of records by a designated person.

(9) The obligations that are imposed on a designated person under this section continue to apply to a person who has been a designated person, but has ceased to carry on business as a designated person.

(10) A requirement for a designated person that is a body corporate to retain any record under this section extends to any body corporate that is a successor to, or a continuation of, the body corporate.

(11) The Minister may make regulations prescribing requirements relating to the retention of records referred to in this section of a body corporate that is wound up or a partnership that is dissolved.

(12) A designated person who fails to comply with this section commits an offence and is liable—

(*a*) on summary conviction, to a fine not exceeding €5,000 or imprisonment for a term not exceeding 12 months (or both), or

(*b*) on conviction on indictment, to a fine or imprisonment for a term not exceeding 5 years (or both).

Section Note

Section 55(1) to (3) requires that certain documents and records be maintained by a designated person. Section 55(4) establishes a five-year retention period in respect of such documents and records (this is consistent with Art.30 of the Directive) and identifies the date from which the five-year period is to be calculated in respect of various records. Of course, Ireland could (by virtue of Art.5 of the Directive) have adopted a more stringent retention period than the five-year period referred to in Art.30, and in fact s.55(4) of the Bill, as introduced, provided for a minimum six-year retention period. However, this was amended in the Seanad to five years and when the Dáil moved to consider the Seanad amendments, the Minister for Justice, Equality and Law Reform contended that the five-year period should be supported by the House as it aligned Ireland to the norm in other Member States. Though the Minister did not mention this, the five-year period also accords with the tenth of the FATF 40 Recommendations (FATF, *FATF 40 Recommendations*, p.7) in this regard. Even so, the five-year period was not universally popular among Dáil deputies. Thus per Deputy Charles Flanagan:

> "As far as some legislation is concerned, six years is the norm. For other professional bodies their duty is to keep records for five years....I thought the Department of Finance, the Department of Justice, Equality and Law Reform or any other Department would strive for an element of consistency in this regard and not have different rules applying in different circumstances in a way that is less than consistent and can give rise to an element of uncertainty or confusion on the part of the service providers and members of the general public". (707(4) *Díospóireachtaí Parlaiminte* (Dáil Éireann) (28.4.10), p.645 *et seq.*).

It is hard not to have a certain sympathy for the points raised by Deputy Flanagan. For example, much of the information gathered or to be gathered under the Act will pertain to consumers within the meaning of the Consumer Protection Code. The term "consumer" in this context encompasses a particularly wide array of individuals, including any of the following:

> "a) a natural person acting outside their business, trade or profession; b) a person or group of persons, but not an

incorporated body with an annual turnover in excess of €3
million...c) incorporated bodies having an annual turnover
of €3 million or less in the financial year (provided that such
body shall not be a member of a group of companies having
a combined turnover greater than the said €3 million); or d) a
member of a credit union; and includes, where appropriate,
a potential "consumer". (Financial Regulator, *Consumer Protection Code* (Dublin: 2006), p. 4).

Category b) above is so wide that it would appear to include any
person other than an incorporated body with an annual turnover in
excess of €3 million, and if such a body happens to be a member of a
credit union it too would be a consumer. Under the Code (Ch.2,
para.49, p.18 *et seq.*), a standard six-year retention period from the
date of a transaction (in the case of an individual transaction) or
otherwise the date on which a relationship ends applies in respect of
consumer "records", *i.e.* "any document, file or information (whether
stored electronically or otherwise) and which is capable of being
reproduced in a legible form" (Consumer Protection Code, p.6). Given
the provisions of s.55(8) of the Act, and assuming that the Consumer
Protection Code is a "rule of law" for the purposes of that section, the
end result is that for a whole swathe of documentation obtained by
regulated entities subject to the Consumer Protection Code, a six-year
retention period applies as standard.

Section 55(9) provides for the continuing application of the record-
retention obligations of s.55 to designated persons who have ceased to
carry on business as a designated person. On a separate but related
note, s.55(10) provides for the continuing application of record-retention
obligations to a body corporate that is a successor to, or continuation of,
a body corporate that is subject to those obligations. Section 55(11)
empowers the Minister for Justice and Law Reform to make regulations
relating to the retention of records of a body corporate that is wound up
or dissolved. At the time of writing, no such regulations have been made
under the Act. Failure by a designated person to comply with s.55 is a
criminal offence (per s.55(12)). (On offences generally under the Act,
see the table of offences arising under the Act (and the penalties for
same) in Appendix 2 of this text).

CHAPTER 7

Special provisions applying to credit and financial institutions

General Note

Ch.7 comprises a miscellany of measures pertaining to credit and
financial institutions. S.56 imposes obligations as regards the provision
of information by such institutions to An Garda Síochána (but not the
Revenue Commissioners). Section 57 is concerned with the application of Chapters II and IV of the Directive to branches/subsidiaries in

non-Member States. Section 58 is concerned with anonymous accounts. S.59 is concerned with relations between credit institutions and "shell banks" (the term is defined in s.59).

Measures for retrieval of information relating to business relationships

56.—(1) A credit institution or financial institution that is a designated person shall have systems in place to enable it to respond fully and promptly to enquiries from the Garda Síochána—

> (*a*) as to whether or not it has, or has had, a business relationship, within the previous 6 years, with a person specified by the Garda Síochána, and
> (*b*) the nature of any such relationship with that person.

(2) A credit institution or financial institution that fails to comply with this section commits an offence and is liable—

> (*a*) on summary conviction, to a fine not exceeding €5,000 or imprisonment for a term not exceeding 12 months (or both), or
> (*b*) on conviction on indictment, to a fine or imprisonment for a term not exceeding 5 years (or both).

General Note:
The reference to a six-year period in s.56(1)(a) sits somewhat uneasily with, for example, s.55(4). It is also more stringent than the relevant provision of the Directive (Art.32), the time-period prescribed thereunder being five years. Failure by a credit/financial institution to comply with s.56 is a criminal offence. (On offences generally under the Act, see the table of offences arising under the Act (and the penalties for same) in Appendix 2 of this text.).

Application of certain requirements to branches and subsidiaries in non-Member States

57.—(1) A credit institution or financial institution that is a designated person and incorporated in the State shall ensure that any branch of the institution, or any subsidiary of the institution that is also a credit institution or financial institution, in a place other than a Member State, applies requirements equivalent to those specified in Chapters II and IV of the Third Money Laundering Directive.

(2) If the place concerned does not permit the application of requirements equivalent to those specified in Chapters II and IV of the Third Money Laundering Directive, the designated person shall—

> (*a*) inform the competent authority for the designated person, and
> (*b*) apply measures, determined in consultation with the competent authority, to deal with the risk of money laundering or terrorist financing arising from the absence of those requirements.

(3) A credit institution or financial institution that is a designated person and incorporated in the State shall communicate any policies and procedures that it has adopted under *section 54* to any branch or subsidiary referred to in *subsection (1)* that is in a place other than a Member State.

(4) A designated person that fails to comply with this section commits an offence and is liable—

(a) on summary conviction, to a fine not exceeding €5,000 or imprisonment for a term not exceeding 12 months (or both), or

(b) on conviction on indictment, to a fine or imprisonment for a term not exceeding 5 years (or both).

Section Note

Section 57 accords with the twenty-second of the FATF 40 Recommendations (FATF, *FATF 40 Recommendations*, p.9). As for Chapters II and IV of the Directive, they are concerned respectively with customer due diligence and record-keeping/statistical data. Notably, s.57 applies only to (a) a branch or (b) a subsidiary that is also a credit institution or a financial institution; it does not extend to a representative office, nor to a subsidiary that is not a credit institution or financial institution. Failure by a designated person to comply with s.57 is a criminal offence (per s.57(4)). (On offences generally under the Act, see the table of offences arising under the Act (and the penalties for same) in Appendix 2 of this text).

Anonymous accounts

58.—(1) A credit institution or financial institution shall not set up an anonymous account for, or provide an anonymous passbook to, any customer.

(2) A credit institution or financial institution shall not keep any anonymous account, or anonymous passbook, that was in existence immediately before the commencement of this section for any customer.

(3) A credit institution or financial institution that fails to comply with this section commits an offence and is liable—

(a) on summary conviction, to a fine not exceeding €5,000 or imprisonment for a term not exceeding 12 months (or both), or

(b) on conviction on indictment, to a fine or imprisonment for a term not exceeding 5 years (or both).

Section Note

Section 58 makes provision in respect of anonymous accounts, more because the Directive requires provision in this regard than because anonymous accounts have been an area of concern in Ireland. As the Minister for Justice, Equality and Law Reform noted during the Second

Stage reading of the Criminal Justice (Money Laundering and Terrorist Financing) Bill 2009:

> "Anonymous or numbered bank accounts or pass-books have not been a feature of the Irish banking system, although they have been a feature in those of some other jurisdictions. (695(2) *Díospóireachtaí Parlaiminte* (Dáil Éireann) (19.11.2009), p.265).

Failure by a credit/financial institution to comply with s.58 is a criminal offence (per s.58(3)). (On offences generally under the Act, see the table of offences arising under the Act (and the penalties for same) in Appendix 2 of this text).

Relationships between credit institutions and shell banks

59.—(1) A credit institution shall not enter into a correspondent banking relationship with a shell bank.

(2) A credit institution that has entered into a correspondent banking relationship with a shell bank before the commencement of this section shall not continue that relationship.

(3) A credit institution shall not engage in or continue a correspondent banking relationship with a bank that the institution knows permits its accounts to be used by a shell bank.

(4) A credit institution shall apply appropriate measures to ensure that it does not enter into or continue a correspondent banking relationship that permits its accounts to be used by a shell bank.

(5) A credit institution that fails to comply with this section commits an offence and is liable—

(*a*) on summary conviction, to a fine not exceeding €5,000 or imprisonment for a term not exceeding 12 months (or both), or

(*b*) on conviction on indictment, to a fine or imprisonment for a term not exceeding 5 years (or both).

(6) In this section, "shell bank" means a credit institution (or a body corporate that is engaged in activities equivalent to a credit institution) that—

(*a*) does not have a physical presence, involving meaningful decision-making and management, in the jurisdiction in which it is incorporated,

(*b*) is not authorised to operate, and is not subject to supervision, as a credit institution (or equivalent) in the jurisdiction in which it is incorporated, and

(*c*) is not affiliated with another body corporate that—

   (i) has a physical presence, involving meaningful decision-making and management, in the jurisdiction in which it is incorporated, and

   (ii) is authorised to operate, and is subject to supervision, as a credit institution or an insurance undertaking, in the jurisdiction in which it is incorporated.

Section Note
The provisions of s.59, which implement Art.13(5) of the Directive, also accord with the eighteenth of the FATF 40 Recommendations (FATF, *FATF 40 Recommendations*, p.9). Failure by a credit institution to comply with s.59 is a criminal offence. (On offences generally under the Act, see the table of offences arising under the Act (and the penalties for same) in Appendix 2 of this text).

CHAPTER 8

Monitoring of designated persons

General Note
Ch.8 provides for the monitoring of designated persons to better ensure compliance with Pt.4 of the Act and for the appointment of authorised officers to assist in this regard.

Competent authorities
Section 60 establishes a "competent authority" for the various classes of designated person with the default competent authority being the Minister for Justice and Law Reform. (The reference in s.60(2)(a) to the Central Bank and Financial Services Authority of Ireland has now been amended to refer to the Central Bank of Ireland (Per the Central Bank Reform Act 2010 (No. 23 of 2010), s.15(14) and Schedule 2, Pt.14)). The term "competent authority" embraces four categories of person, namely the Central Bank, certain professional regulatory bodies, the Minister for Justice and Law Reform and any prescribed entity. S.60(2)(b) (in part) and (c) to (e) accords with the twenty-fourth of the FATF Recommendations which recommends that:

> "Countries should ensure that the other categories of designated non-financial businesses and professions are subject to effective systems for monitoring and ensuring their compliance with requirements to combat money-laundering and terrorist financing. This should be performed on a risk-sensitive basis. This may be performed by a government authority or by an appropriate self-regulatory organisation, provided that such an organisation can ensure that its members comply with their obligations to combat money laundering and terrorist financing." (FATF, *FATF 40 Recommendations*, p.10).

There is no express reference in the Act to monitoring being done on a risk-sensitive basis, though it is perhaps possible to read the requirement imposed on competent authorities by s.63(1) to "effectively monitor" designated persons as moderating the obligations of competent authorities in this regard given that what is effective in one context may be more or less rigorous to what is required in another context depending on the money laundering/terrorist financing risk arising.

Section 61 makes provisions regarding for agreements between competent authorities as to which shall be the competent authority for a designated person who comes within the remit of more than one competent authority. Section 62 provides for the establishment of a category of competent authorities known as State competent authorities. (The reference in s.62(1)(a) to the Central Bank and Financial Services Authority of Ireland has now been amended to refer to the Central Bank of Ireland (Per the Central Bank Reform Act 2010 (No. 23 of 2010), s.15(14) and Schedule 2, Pt.14)). Section 63 prescribes what a competent authority is to do. Its responsibilities are effectively threefold: to effectively monitor those designated persons that come within its remit; to take such measures as are reasonably necessary to secure compliance by those persons with Pt.4; and to report to An Garda Síochána and the Revenue Commissioners any knowledge or suspicion of the competent authority that a designated person or another person has been or is engaged in money laundering or terrorist financing. Section 64 makes clear that the role entrusted to a competent authority in Pt.4 does not restrict any functions that it has under any enactment or rule of law. Section 65 requires a competent authority to include a section in its annual report concerning the activities it carried out in performing its functions under the Act for the year to which the annual report relates. Section 66 empowers a State competent authority to seek such "relevant information" of certain prescribed bodies (such as public bodies and representative, regulatory, licensing and registration authorities) as is reasonably required by the State competent authority in carrying out its functions under Pt.4. Section 67 empowers a State competent authority to direct a designated person for whom that State competent authority is a competent authority, to provide such information or documents (or both) relating to the designated person as the authority may specify by notice in writing. S.68 empowers a State competent authority also to direct a designated person to furnish to the authority an explanation of certain documents relating to that designated person. Section 69 constrains the powers of State competent authorities under ss.67 and 68 allowing such authorities to issue a s.67/68 direction only in relation to information or documents reasonably required by the authority to assist it to perform its functions under Pt.4. Section 70 offers protection against self-incrimination in the context of directions made under s.67 or 68. Section 71 provides that a State competent authority may, by notice in writing, direct a designated person, within such reasonable time as it shall specify, to discontinue or refrain from engaging in specified conduct that in the opinion of that authority constitutes (or, if engaged in, would constitute) a breach of any specified provision of Pt.4.

Authorised officers

Section 72 provides for the appointment of authorised officers for the purpose of Ch.8. Section 73 requires that every such authorised officer be furnished with a warrant of appointment as same. Section 74 empowers each such authorised officer to exercise powers only for the purpose of assisting the appointing State competent authority to perform its functions under Pt.4. Section 75 empowers an authorised officer to enter certain premises. Section 76 makes clear that nothing in Ch.8 empowers an authorised officer to enter a residential premises without either the permission of the occupier or a warrant. Section 77 provides what an authorised officer may do at any premises lawfully entered by that officer. Section 78 makes provision as to the issuance of a District Court warrant to an authorised officer to enter into premises and do certain things there. Section 79 provides who may accompany and assist an authorised officer when the latter is exercising powers under a warrant issued under s.78. Section 80 makes it an offence where a person, without reasonable excuse: obstructs or interferes with an authorised officer in the exercise of his powers under Ch.8; or fails to comply with a defined requirement or request of such an officer (the reference to authorised officer including such persons as accompany and assist him or her in accordance with s.79).

Preservation of certain rights
It will be recalled that s.70 offers protection against self-incrimination in the context of directions made under s.67 or 68. Sections 81 to 83 make separate but not entirely dissimilar provision. Thus s.81 provides that nothing in Ch.8 requires a person to answer questions if to do so might tend to incriminate that person. Section 82 provides that nothing in Ch.8 requires the production of any document or information subject to legal privilege. Section 83, considered in the context of s.7(7) above, provides that disclosure or production of any information/documents by any person in accordance with Ch.8 shall not be treated as a breach of any restriction on disclosure or production imposed by any enactment or rule of law on the person making the disclosure or production (or the person on whose behalf such disclosure or production is done); nor shall production of any item forming part of the documents relating to the business of a designated person prejudice any lien claimed over same.

Meaning of "competent authority"

60.—(1) Subject to *section 61*, a reference in this Part to the competent authority for a designated person is a reference to the competent authority prescribed for the class of designated persons to which the designated person belongs.

(2) If no such competent authority is prescribed, a reference in this Part to the competent authority is a reference to the following:

(a) in the case of a designated person that is a credit institution or a financial institution, the Central Bank and Financial Services Authority of Ireland;

(b) in the case of a designated person who is an auditor, external accountant, tax adviser or trust or company service provider—

(i) if the person is a member of a designated accountancy body, the designated accountancy body, or

(ii) if the person is not a member of a designated accountancy body and is a body corporate, or a body of unincorporated persons, carrying out its functions under this Part through officers, members or employees of it who are members of a designated accountancy body, the designated accountancy body;

(c) in the case of a designated person who is a solicitor, the Law Society of Ireland;

(d) in the case of a designated person who is a barrister, the General Council of the Bar of Ireland;

(e) in the case of any designated person other than a designated person referred to in *paragraph (a), (b), (c)* or *(d)*, the Minister.

(3) The Minister may prescribe a competent authority for a class of designated persons, for the purpose of *subsection (1)*, only if the Minister is satisfied that the competent authority is more appropriate than the competent authority specified in *subsection (2)* for the class of designated persons, having regard to the nature of the business activities engaged in by that class.

Agreements between competent authorities where more than one applicable

61.—(1) Where there is more than one competent authority for a designated person under *section 60*, those competent authorities may agree that one of them will act as the competent authority for that person, and references in this Part to a competent authority are to be construed accordingly.

(2) An agreement under this section, in relation to a designated person, takes effect when the competent authority who has agreed to act as the competent authority for the designated person gives notice, in writing, to that person.

(3) An agreement under this section, in relation to a designated person, ceases to have effect when—

(a) any of the parties to the agreement gives notice, in writing, to the other parties of the termination of the agreement,

(b) the agreement expires, or

(c) as a result of the operation of *section 60(1)*, the competent authority who has agreed to act as the competent authority is no longer a competent authority of the person under *section 60*, whichever is the earliest.

Meaning of "State competent authority"

62.—(1) In this Part, a reference to a State competent authority is a reference to one of the following competent authorities:

(*a*) the Central Bank and Financial Services Authority of Ireland;

(*b*) the Minister;

(*c*) such other competent authority as is prescribed.

(2) The Minister may prescribe a competent authority as a State competent authority for the purposes of *subsection (1)(c)* only if—

(*a*) the Minister is satisfied that the competent authority is appropriate, having regard to the functions of State competent authorities under this Part, and

(*b*) the competent authority is a Minister of the Government or an officer of a particular class or description of a Department of State or is a body (not being a company) by or under an enactment.

Section Note

At the time of writing no further competent authority has been prescribed by the Minister for Justice and Law Reform as a "State competent authority".

General functions of competent authorities

63.—(1) A competent authority shall effectively monitor the designated persons for whom it is a competent authority and take measures that are reasonably necessary for the purpose of securing compliance by those designated persons with the requirements specified in this Part.

(2) The measures that are reasonably necessary include reporting to the Garda Síochána and Revenue Commissioners any knowledge or suspicion that the competent authority has that a designated person has been or is engaged in money laundering or terrorist financing.

(3) In determining, in any particular case, whether a designated person has complied with any of the requirements specified in this Part, a competent authority shall consider whether the person is able to demonstrate to the competent authority that the requirements have been met.

(4) A competent authority that, in the course of monitoring a designated person under this section, acquires any knowledge or forms any suspicion that another person has been or is engaged in money laundering or terrorist financing shall report that knowledge or suspicion to the Garda Síochána and Revenue Commissioners.

Section Note

There are perhaps four points of particular note as regards this provision. First, the reference to "effective monitoring" by a competent authority, the significance of this requirement having been already considered in the General Note to Ch.8 above. Second, the reference in s.63(1) to a monitoring authority taking such measures as are "reasonably necessary" for the purpose of securing compliance by a designated person with the requirements of Pt.4. It remains to be seen what measures (other than the reporting requirement referred to in s.63(2)) the various competent authorities will consider to be "reasonably necessary"; the phrase would appear to have both an empowering and a restraining effect on their actions. Third, the requirement in s.63(3) that a competent authority, in determining whether a designated person has complied with any requirements of Pt.4, consider whether such person is able to demonstrate to the competent authority that the requirements have been met. This effectively establishes an indirect obligation for designated persons to document their compliance with Pt.4 in such manner as to be able to demonstrate their compliance with that Part to the relevant competent authority. Fourth, the obligation on a competent authority to report to the Garda Síochána and the Revenue Commissioners any knowledge or suspicion of the competent authority that a designated person or another person has been or is engaged in money laundering or terrorist financing (s.63(2) and (4)). This last obligation is not entirely dissimilar to that which existed under s.57(2) of the Criminal Justice Act 1994, though there are differences. Both that (largely repealed) provision and s.63 of the Act respectively have the effect of casting the relationship of competent authority and monitored party in a particular mould.

Application of other enactments

64.—Nothing in this Part limits any functions that a competent authority (including a State competent authority) has under any other enactment or rule of law.

Annual reporting

65.—A competent authority shall include, in each annual report published by the authority, an account of the activities that it has carried out in performing its functions under this Act during the year to which the annual report relates.

Section Note

The year 2010 is the first year in which this obligation arises and, at the time of writing, the extent to which competent authorities will detail the activities referred to in this section remains to be seen.

Request to bodies to provide names, addresses and other information relating to designated persons

66.—(1) In this section, a reference to relevant information, in relation to a person, that is held by a body is a reference to any of the following information that is held by the body:

(*a*) the name, address or other contact details of the person;

(*b*) any other prescribed information relating to the person.

(2) A State competent authority may, by notice in writing, request any public body, or any body that represents, regulates or licenses, registers or otherwise authorises persons carrying on any trade, profession, business or employment, to provide the authority with any relevant information, in relation to—

(*a*) any designated persons for whom the authority is a competent authority, or

(*b*) any persons whom the body reasonably considers may be such designated persons.

(3) A State competent authority may make a request under this section only in relation to information that is reasonably required by the authority to assist the authority in carrying out its functions under this Part.

(4) Notwithstanding any other enactment or rule of law, a body that receives a request under this section shall disclose the relevant information concerned.

(5) The Minister may prescribe information, for the purposes of *subsection (1)(b)*, that a State competent authority may request under this section only if the Minister is satisfied that the information is appropriate, having regard to the functions of the State competent authority under this Part.

Direction to furnish information or documents

67.—(1) A State competent authority may, by notice in writing, direct a designated person for whom the authority is a competent authority to provide such information or documents (or both) relating to the designated person specified in the notice.

(2) A person who, without reasonable excuse, fails to comply with a direction under this section commits an offence and is liable, on summary conviction, to a fine not exceeding €5,000 or imprisonment for a term not exceeding 12 months (or both).

(3) In giving a direction under this section, a State competent authority shall specify the manner in which any document or information is required to be furnished and a reasonable time by which the document or information is required to be furnished.

(4) A person is required to furnish documents in accordance with this section only if the documents are in the person's possession or within the person's power to obtain lawfully.

(5) If a person knows the whereabouts of documents to which the direction applies, the person shall furnish to the State competent authority who gave the direction a statement, verified by a statutory declaration, identifying the whereabouts of the documents. The person shall furnish the statement no later than the time by which the direction specifies that the documents are required to be furnished.

(6) A person who, without reasonable excuse, fails to comply with *subsection (5)* commits an offence and is liable, on summary conviction, to

a fine not exceeding €5,000 or imprisonment for a term not exceeding 12 months (or both).

(7) If any document required to be furnished under this section is in electronic, mechanical or other form, the document shall be furnished in written form, unless the direction specifies otherwise.

(8) A State competent authority may take copies of, or extracts from, any document furnished to the authority under this section.

Direction to provide explanation of documents

68.—(1) A State competent authority may, by notice in writing, direct a designated person for whom the authority is a competent authority to furnish to the authority an explanation of any documents relating to the designated person that—

- (*a*) the person has furnished to the authority in complying with a direction under *section 67*, or
- (*b*) an authorised officer has lawfully removed from premises under *section 77* (including as applied by *section 78*).

(2) In giving a direction under this section, a State competent authority shall specify the manner in which any explanation of a document is required to be furnished and a reasonable time by which the explanation is required to be furnished.

(3) A person who, without reasonable excuse, fails to comply with a direction under this section commits an offence and is liable, on summary conviction, to a fine not exceeding €5,000 or imprisonment for a term not exceeding 12 months (or both).

Purpose of direction under section 67 *or* 68

69.—A State competent authority may give a direction under *section 67* or *68* only in relation to information or documents reasonably required by the authority to assist the authority to perform its functions under this Part.

Self-incrimination (sections 67 *and* 68)

70.—Nothing in *section 67* or *68* requires a person to comply with a direction under the section concerned to furnish any information if to do so might tend to incriminate the person.

Direction to designated person to comply with obligations under this Part

71.—(1) A State competent authority may, by notice in writing, direct a designated person for whom the authority is a competent authority to discontinue, or refrain from engaging in, specified conduct that in the opinion of the authority constitutes, or, if engaged in, would constitute, a breach of any specified provision of this Part.

(2) The State competent authority shall specify in the direction a reasonable time by which the direction is to be complied with.

(3) If the designated person fails to comply with the direction and is subsequently found guilty of an offence consisting of the conduct specified in the direction, the court shall take the failure to comply with the direction into account as an aggravating factor in determining any sentence to be imposed on the person for the offence.

Section Note
It seems unlikely that a State competent authority would lightly issue a notice under s.71. At the very least the State competent authority would need to have formed the opinion that specified conduct constitutes or, if engaged in, would constitute, a breach of a provision of Pt.4. Its forming this opinion seems unlikely generally to come as a complete surprise to the affected designated person as one would expect that a State competent authority, provided it is not also a designated person, would typically have trailed its thinking in advance with the relevant designated person. If a State competent authority was also a designated person it would of course need to be careful in this regard that it did not commit the offence of tipping off. The requirement in sub-s.(2) that the State competent authority specify a "reasonable time" in the direction for compliance with same affords a possible ground of challenge to the direction by an affected designated person, namely that the time specified was not reasonable. For this reason it can perhaps be expected, and would certainly seem prudent, that a State competent authority err on the side of generosity when determining this "reasonable time". Failure to comply with a s.71 direction, where followed by a conviction for the offence specified in the direction, is a serious matter: the relevant court must take the failure to comply with the direction into account as an aggravating factor when imposing sentence (per s.71(3)). The possibility that a criminal prosecution will occur in relation to actual conduct that prompts the issuance of a s.71 direction is likely bolstered by the reporting obligation that arises for competent authorities under s.63 of the Act (considered above); after all, where a s.71 direction issues a State competent authority seems likely to find itself in, or teetering on, a situation where a report to the Garda Síochána and the Revenue Commissioners may be mandatory.

Appointment of authorised officers

72.—(1) A State competent authority may appoint employees of the authority or other persons who, in the opinion of the authority, are suitably qualified or experienced, to be authorised officers for the purpose of this Chapter.

(2) A State competent authority may revoke any appointment made by the authority under *subsection (1)*.

(3) An appointment or revocation under this section shall be in writing.

(4) A person's appointment by a State competent authority as an authorised officer ceases—

(*a*) on the revocation by the authority of the appointment,

(b) in a case where the appointment is for a specified period, on the expiration of the period,

(c) on the person's resignation from the appointment, or

(d) in a case where the person is an employee of the authority—

    (i) on the resignation of the person as an employee of the authority, or

    (ii) on the termination of the person's employment with the authority for any other reason.

Warrant of appointment

73.—(1) Every authorised officer appointed by a State competent authority shall be furnished with a warrant of appointment as an authorised officer by the State competent authority.

(2) In the course of performing the functions of an authorised officer under this Chapter, the officer shall, if requested to do so by any person affected, produce the officer's warrant of appointment for inspection.

Powers may only be exercised for assisting State competent authority

74.—An authorised officer may exercise powers as an authorised officer under this Chapter only for the purpose of assisting the State competent authority that appointed the authorised officer in the performance of the authority's functions under this Part.

General power of authorised officers to enter premises

75.—(1) An authorised officer may enter any premises at which the authorised officer reasonably believes that the business of a designated person has been or is carried on.

(2) An authorised officer may enter any premises at which the authorised officer reasonably believes records or other documents relating to the business of a designated person are located.

(3) An authorised officer may enter premises under *subsection (1)* or *(2)*—

(a) in a case where the authorised officer reasonably believes that the business of a designated person is carried on at the premises (as referred to in *subsection (1)*), at any time during which the authorised officer reasonably believes that the business is being carried on there, or

(b) in any other case, at any reasonable time.

Entry into residential premises only with permission or warrant

76.—Nothing in this Chapter shall be construed as empowering an authorised officer to enter any dwelling without the permission of the occupier or the authority of a warrant under *section 78*.

Power of authorised officers to do things at premises

77.—(1) An authorised officer may, at any premises lawfully entered by the officer, do any of the following:

(a) inspect the premises;

(b) request any person on the premises who apparently has control of, or access to, records or other documents that relate to the business of a designated person (being a designated person whose competent authority is the State competent authority who appointed the authorised officer)—

    (i) to produce the documents for inspection, and

    (ii) if any of those documents are in an electronic, mechanical or other form, to reproduce the document in a written form;

(c) inspect documents produced or reproduced in accordance with such a request or found in the course of inspecting the premises;

(d) take copies of those documents or of any part of them (including, in the case of a document in an electronic, mechanical or other form, a copy of the document in a written form);

(e) request any person at the premises who appears to the authorised person to have information relating to the documents, or to the business of the designated person, to answer questions with respect to the documents or that business;

(f) remove and retain the documents (including in the case of a document in an electronic, mechanical or other form, a copy of the information in a written form) for the period reasonably required for further examination;

(g) request a person who has charge of, operates or is concerned in the operation of data equipment, including any person who has operated that equipment, to give the officer all reasonable assistance in relation to the operation of the equipment or access to the data stored within it;

(h) secure, for later inspection, the premises or part of the premises at which the authorised officer reasonably believes records or other documents relating to the business of the designated person are located.

(2) A person to whom a request is made in accordance with *subsection (1)* shall—

(a) comply with the request so far as it is possible to do so, and

(b) give such other assistance and information to the authorised officer with respect to the business of the designated person concerned as is reasonable in the circumstances.

(3) A reference in this section to data equipment includes a reference to any associated apparatus.

(4) A reference in this section to a person who operates or has operated data equipment includes a reference to a person on whose behalf data equipment is operated or has been operated.

Entry to premises and doing of things under warrant

78.—(1) A judge of the District Court may issue a warrant under this section if satisfied, by information on oath of an authorised officer, that there are reasonable grounds for believing that—

(*a*) documents relating to the business of a designated person that are required for the purpose of assisting the State competent authority that appointed the authorised officer under this Chapter in the performance of the authority's functions under this Part are contained on premises, and

(*b*) the premises comprise a dwelling or an authorised officer has been obstructed or otherwise prevented from entering the premises under *section 75.*

(2) A warrant under this section authorises an authorised officer, at any time or times within one month of the issue of the warrant—

(*a*) to enter the premises specified in the warrant, and

(*b*) to exercise the powers conferred on authorised officers by this Chapter or any of those powers that are specified in the warrant.

(3) Entry to premises the subject of a warrant may be effected with the use of reasonable force.

Section Note

Section 78 refers to the provision of information "on oath". (s.17(2) contains a similar reference). At the Report and Final Stage reading by the Dáil of the Bill, the Labour Party tabled an amendment which would have seen the words "or affirmation" inserted after "oath". Technically the amendment was unnecessary as s.21 (coupled with the Schedule) of the Interpretation Act 2005 makes clear that a statutory reference to an oath, in the case of a person for the time being allowed by law to affirm or declare, includes an affirmation or declaration. However, the Labour Party considered it preferable to insert the alternative directly into the Bill rather than rely on a rule of statutory interpretation to introduce the alternative. The proposed amendment was not accepted by the Government, the Minister for Justice, Equality and Law Reform stating in this regard:

> "The Interpretation Act 2005 already provides that the word "oath", in the case of a person for the time being allowed by law to affirm or declare, includes an affirmation or declaration. We do not believe it is preferable to define something in a Bill or Act if it has already been dealt with in the 2005 Act. In any event, if we were to accept the amendment it would be necessary to amend section 17(2), which deals with information given on oath by a member of the Garda Síochána to a District Court judge in regard to an order to suspend a service or transaction. The Oaths Act 1888 allows a person to make an affirmation instead of an oath in all cases where the oath is required by law." (702(3) *Díospóireachtaí Parlaiminte* (Dáil Éireann) (17.2.2010), p.572).

The same proposed amendment was made (and rejected) at the Committee stage and also the Report and Final stages of the Seanad's consideration of the Bill. (See (201(9) *Díospóireachtaí Parlaiminte*

(Seanad Éireann) (11.3.10), p.597 *et seq.* and 202(2) *Díospóireachtaí Parlaiminte* (Seanad Éireann) (21.4.10), p.79 *et seq*).

Authorised officer may be accompanied by others

79.—An authorised officer may be accompanied, and assisted in the exercise of the officer's powers (including under a warrant issued under *section 78*), by such other authorised officers, members of the Garda Síochána or other persons as the authorised officer reasonably considers appropriate.

Offence to obstruct, interfere or fail to comply with request

80.—(1) A person commits an offence if the person, without reasonable excuse—

(*a*) obstructs or interferes with an authorised officer in the exercise of the officer's powers under this Chapter, or

(*b*) fails to comply with a requirement, or request made by an authorised officer, under *section 77* (including as applied by *section 78*).

(2) A person who commits an offence under this section is liable, on summary conviction, to a fine not exceeding €5,000 or imprisonment for a term not exceeding 12 months (or both).

(3) A reference in this section to an authorised officer includes a member of the Garda Síochána or other person who is accompanying and assisting the officer in accordance with *section 79*.

Self-incrimination – questions of authorised officers

81.—Nothing in this Chapter requires a person to answer questions if to do so might tend to incriminate the person.

Production of documents or information not required in certain circumstances

82.—Nothing in this Chapter requires the production of any document or information subject to legal privilege.

Disclosure or production not to be treated as breach or to affect lien

83.—(1) The disclosure or production of any information or document by a person in accordance with this Chapter shall not be treated as a breach of any restriction under any enactment or rule of law on disclosure or production by the person or any other person on whose behalf the information or document is disclosed or produced.

(2) The production referred to in *subsection (1)* of any item forming part of the documents relating to the business of a designated person shall not prejudice any lien that the designated person or any other person claims over that item.

CHAPTER 9

Authorisation of Trust or Company Service Providers

General Note

Recital (15) to the Directive states that "As the tightening of controls in the financial sector has prompted money launderers and terrorist financers to seek alternative methods for concealing the origin of the proceeds of crime and as such channels can be used for terrorist financing, the anti-money laundering and anti-terrorist financing obligations should cover life insurance intermediaries and trust and company service providers". Art.36 of the Directive requires, *inter alia*, that trust and company service providers be licensed or registered. (The term "trust and company service providers" in the Directive has been changed into "trust or company service provider" in the Act). S.87(1) of the Act makes it an offence for a person to carry on business as a "trust or company service provider" without being the holder of an authorisation issued by the Minister for Justice and Law Reform under Ch.9. Ch.9 is largely concerned with establishing a new regulatory régime for such persons.

What is a "trust or company service provider"?
Section 24(1) defines a "trust or company service provider" as any person whose business it is to provide any of the following services: (1) forming companies or other bodies corporate; (2) acting as a director/ secretary of a company under an arrangement with a person other than the company; (3) arranging for another person to act as a director/ secretary of a company; (4) acting, or arranging for a person to act, as a partner of a partnership; (5) providing a registered office, business address, correspondence or administrative address or other related services for a body corporate or partnership; (6) acting, or arranging for another person to act, as a trustee of a trust; (7) acting, or arranging for another person to act, as a nominee shareholder for a person other than a company whose securities are listed on a regulated market. Any entity that provides *e.g.* company secretarial services would come within this definition. However, the definition is very wide-reaching and may extend to some entities that would not necessarily think themselves (at least in layman's terms) to be a "trust or company service provider". For example, executive recruitment firms arrange for other persons to act as a director/secretary of a company and it might be queried whether this would suffice to bring such entities within the third limb of the definition of "trust or company service provider". Section 84 of the Act excludes the following persons from the definition of "trust or company service provider" for the purposes of Ch.9: a member of a designated accountancy body; a practising barrister; a practising solicitor; a credit institution; and a financial institution. Thus a reference in Ch.9 of Pt.4 of the Act to a "trust or company service provider" is a reference to such an entity as defined in s.24(1) of the Act (as expanded upon by s.84),

whereas a reference elsewhere in the Act to a "trust or company service provider" is to such an entity as defined in s.24(1).

Summary of key elements of Ch.9
Section 88 of the Act makes provision for the application for authorisation to carry on business as a trust or company service provider by an individual, body corporate or partnership. (Under the Trust or Company Service Provider (Authorisation) (Fees) Regulations 2010 (S.I. No. 348 of 2010), the Minister for Justice and Law Reform has prescribed €130 as the fee that must accompany an application made under s.88). Section 89 makes provision as regards the granting/refusal (principally the refusal) of such applications by the Minister for Justice and Law Reform. Section 90 empowers the Minister for Justice and Law Reform to impose conditions when granting an application for an authorisation. Section 91 makes provision as regards the commencement and duration of an authorisation (the standard duration being three years). Section 92 provides for the renewal by the Minister for Justice and Law Reform of a (non-revoked) authorisation. (Under the Trust or Company Service Provider (Authorisation) (Fees) Regulations 2010 (S.I. No. 348 of 2010), the Minister for Justice and Law Reform has prescribed €130 as the fee that must accompany an application made under s.92 of the Act). Section 93 empowers the Minister for Justice and Law Reform, in defined circumstances, to amend an authorisation granted under Ch.9. Under s.94, failure by an authorisation-holder to comply with any condition of the relevant authorisation or any prescribed requirements is an offence, punishable by fine only. Section 95 requires that an authorisation-holder take reasonable steps to ensure that each of certain senior staff within, as well as any beneficial owner of, the authorisation-holder is a "fit and proper person" (what does not constitute a "fit and proper person" is set out in s.85). Section 96 empowers the Minister for Justice and Law Reform to revoke an authorisation on the application of an authorisation-holder; s.97 makes provision for revocation other than on the application of an authorisation-holder. Section 98 empowers the Minister for Justice and Law Reform, where s/he believes that there may be grounds for revoking an authorisation under s.97, to prohibit an authorisation-holder from carrying on business as a trust or company service provider other than in accordance with conditions specified by the Minister. Section 99 makes provision as regards the publication by the Minister for Justice and Law Reform of an official notice giving particulars of a revocation (under s.96 or 97) or a direction (under s.98). Section 100 makes provision for an appeal to be made against various decisions of the Minister under Ch.9 to an Appeal Tribunal, one or more of which Tribunals falls to be established under s.101. Section 102 empowers the Minister to request of the Garda Commissioner any information that is required to assist the Minister in determining, for the purposes of Ch.9, whether any of certain persons is a "fit and proper person". Section 103 empowers the Minister for Justice and Law Reform to perform those functions given a State competent authority in Ch.8 in order to assist

him/her in carrying out the functions conferred by Ch.9 in relation to trust or company service providers and makes certain related provision. Section 104 requires the Minister to establish and maintain, at an office of the Department of Justice and Law Reform, a register of persons authorised to carry on business as a trust or company service provider, and makes certain related provision. Under s.105 of the Act, at least once every twelve months from 15 July 2010, the Minister must publish a list of persons holding authorisations and any (if any) prescribed particulars in *Iris Oifigiúil*. Section 106 requires an authorisation-holder to retain certain records.

Interpretation (*Chapter 9*)

84.—In this Chapter—

"Appeal Tribunal" means an Appeal Tribunal established under *section 101*;

"authorisation" means an authorisation to carry on business as a trust or company service provider granted under this Chapter and, if such an authorisation is renewed or amended under this Chapter, means, unless the context otherwise requires, the authorisation as renewed or amended (as the case may be);

"principal officer" means—

(*a*) in relation to a body corporate, any person who is a director, manager, secretary or other similar officer of the body corporate or any person purporting to act in such a capacity, or

(*b*) in relation to a partnership—

(i) any person who is a partner in, or a manager or other similar officer of, the partnership or any person purporting to act in such a capacity, and

(ii) in a case where a partner of the partnership is a body corporate, any person who is a director, manager, secretary or other similar officer of such a partner or any person purporting to act in such a capacity;

"trust or company service provider" does not include any of the following:

(*a*) a member of a designated accountancy body;

(*b*) a barrister or solicitor;

(*c*) a credit institution or financial institution.

Meaning of "fit and proper person"

85.—For the purposes of this Chapter, a person is not a fit and proper person if any of the following apply:

(*a*) the person has been convicted of any of the following offences:

(i) money laundering;

(ii) terrorist financing;

(iii) an offence involving fraud, dishonesty or breach of trust;

(iv) an offence in respect of conduct in a place other than the State that would constitute an offence of a kind referred to in *subparagraph (i)*, *(ii)* or *(iii)* if the conduct occurred in the State;

(b) in a case where the person is an individual, the person is under 18 years of age;

(c) the person—

(i)   has suspended payments due to the person's creditors,

(ii) is unable to meet other obligations to the person's creditors, or

(iii) is an individual who is an undischarged bankrupt;

(d) the person is otherwise not a fit and proper person.

Authorisations held by partnerships

86.—(1) A reference in a relevant document to the holder or proposed holder of an authorisation includes, in a case where the holder or proposed holder is a partnership, a reference to each partner of the partnership unless otherwise specified.

(2) A reference in *subsection (1)* to a relevant document is a reference to any of the following:

(a) this Chapter;

(b) a regulation made for the purposes of this Chapter;

(c) an authorisation or condition of an authorisation;

(d) any notice or direction given under this Chapter;

(e) any determination under this Chapter.

(3) Without prejudice to the generality of *subsection (1)* or *section 111*, where any requirement is imposed by or under this Chapter on the holder of an authorisation and failure to comply with the requirement is an offence, each partner of a partnership (being a partnership that is the holder of an authorisation) who contravenes the requirement is liable for the offence.

Prohibition on carrying on business of trust or company service provider without authorisation

87.—(1) A person commits an offence if the person carries on business as a trust or company service provider without being the holder of an authorisation issued by the Minister under this Chapter.

(2) A person who commits an offence under *subsection (1)* is liable—

(a) on summary conviction, to a fine not exceeding €5,000, or imprisonment for a term not exceeding 12 months (or both), or

(b) on conviction on indictment, to a fine or imprisonment not exceeding 5 years (or both).

Application for authorisation

88.—(1) An individual, body corporate or partnership may apply to the Minister for an authorisation to carry on business as a trust or company service provider.

(2) The application shall—

(*a*) be in a form provided or specified by the Minister,

(*b*) specify the name of—
    (i) the proposed holder of the authorisation,
    (ii) in a case where the proposed holder of the authorisation is a body corporate or partnership or an individual who proposes to carry on business as a trust or company service provider as a partner in a partnership, any principal officer of the body corporate or partnership (as the case may be), and
    (iii) any person who is, or is proposed to be, a beneficial owner of the business,

(*c*) be accompanied by any consent, in the form provided or specified by the Minister, that is required to enable access to personal data (within the meaning of the Data Protection Acts 1988 and 2003) held by other persons or bodies and that is required to assist the Minister in determining, for the purposes of *section 89* (including as applied by *section 92*) whether or not the proposed holder and other persons referred to in *paragraph (b)* are fit and proper persons,

(*d*) contain such other information, and be accompanied by such documents, as the Minister requests,

(*e*) be accompanied by the prescribed fee (if any).

(3) The Minister may, by written notice given to an applicant, require the applicant to provide, within the period of not less than 14 days specified in the notice, such additional information and documents as are reasonably necessary to enable the Minister to determine the application.

(4) As soon as practicable after an applicant becomes aware that any information or document provided to the Minister under this section contains a material inaccuracy or has changed in any material particular, including information or a document provided in relation to an application that has been granted, but not including information or a document provided in relation to an application that has been refused, the applicant shall give notice in writing to the Minister of the error or change in circumstances, as the case may be.

(5) For the purposes of *subsection (2)(e)* (including as applied by *section 92*), the Minister may prescribe different fees, to accompany applications for authorisations under this Chapter, for different classes of proposed holders of those authorisations and in prescribing such fees may differentiate between the fee to accompany such an application for an authorisation (not being an application for the renewal of such an authorisation) and the fee to accompany an application for the renewal of such an authorisation.

Section Note

At the time of writing, the Minister for Justice and Law Reform has introduced by way of the European Communities (Trust or Company Service Providers) (Temporary Authorisation) Regulations 2010 (S.I. No. 347 of 2010) certain transitional measures that streamline the initial authorisation application process. The Regulations apply to any person who is a trust or company service provider (per regulation 4). They further provide that a person to whom the Regulations apply and who makes an application for an authorisation under s.88 of the Act shall, subject to the provisions of the Regulations, be deemed to enjoy a "temporary authorisation" which shall be an authorisation for the purposes of Ch.9 (per regulation 5). However, a person who has made a previous application under s.88 that has been determined (*i.e.* either refused or granted by the Minister (per regulation 3)) does not become a temporary authorisation-holder by making a further application under s.88 (per regulation 6). A temporary authorisation: (1) comes into effect on the later of (a) the day on which the relevant s.88 application is received by the Minister or (b) 15 July 2010; and (2) ceases to have effect on the earlier of (a) the day on which the relevant application is determined or (b) 30 November 2010 (per regulations 7 and 8). The holder of a temporary authorisation is subject to Ch.9 in the same way as if the temporary authorisation had been granted under that Chapter (per regulation 9); moreover a temporary authorisation may be subject to any prescribed requirements referred to in s.94 of the Act (per regulation 10). Section 104 of the Act requires the Minister to establish and maintain a register of persons authorised to carry on business as a trust or company service provider, the Regulations empower the Minister to establish and maintain (though not necessarily at an office of the Department of Justice and Law Reform) a register of temporary authorisations which in force pursuant to the Regulations, which register the Minister may publish and make available to the public on such conditions as the Minister considers appropriate (regulation 11). Unless the Regulations are amended or substituted, no temporary authorisations will extend in duration beyond 30 November 2010 (regulation 8) and the Regulations will largely cease to be of practical relevance at that time.

Grant and refusal of applications for authorisation

89.—(1) The Minister may refuse an application under *section 88* only if—

    (*a*) the application does not comply with the requirements of *section 88*,

    (*b*) the applicant does not provide any additional documents or information in accordance with a notice given under *section 88(3)*,

    (*c*) the Minister has reasonable grounds to be satisfied that information given to the Minister by the applicant in connection with the application is false or misleading in any material particular,

    (*d*) the Minister has reasonable grounds to be satisfied that any of the following persons is not a fit and proper person:

      (i) the proposed holder of the authorisation;

      (ii) in a case where the proposed holder of the authorisation is a body corporate or partnership or an individual who proposes to carry on business as a trust or company service provider as a partner in a partnership, any principal officer of the body corporate or partnership (as the case may be);

      (iii) any person who is, or is proposed to be, a beneficial owner of the business concerned,

(*e*) the applicant has failed to satisfy the Minister that the proposed holder of the authorisation will comply with the obligations imposed on trust or company service providers, as designated persons, under this Part,

(*f*) the applicant has failed to satisfy the Minister that the proposed holder of the authorisation will comply with each of the following:

      (i) any conditions that the Minister would have imposed on the authorisation concerned if the Minister had granted the application;

      (ii) any prescribed requirements referred to in *section 94*;

      (iii) *section 95*;

      (iv) *section 98*;

      (v) *section 106*,

(*g*) the proposed holder of the authorisation is so structured, or the business of the proposed holder is so organised, that the proposed holder is not capable of being regulated under this Chapter, or as a designated person under this Part, to the satisfaction of the Minister,

(*h*) in a case where the proposed holder of the authorisation is a body corporate, the body corporate is being wound up,

(*i*) in a case where the proposed holder of the authorisation is a partnership, the partnership is dissolved by the death or bankruptcy of a partner or because of the operation of a provision of the Partnership Act 1890 or otherwise,

(*j*) in a case where any person referred to in *paragraph (d)* has been authorised to carry on business as a trust or company service provider in another Member State, an authority of the other Member State that performs functions similar to those of the Minister under this Chapter has terminated the authority of the person to carry on business as a trust or company service provider in the other Member State, or

(*k*) in a case where the proposed holder of the authorisation is a subsidiary of a body corporate that is authorised to carry on business as a trust or company service provider in another Member State, an authority of the other Member State that performs functions similar to those of the Minister under this Chapter has terminated the authority of the body corporate to carry on business as a trust or company service provider in the other Member State.

(2) If the Minister proposes to refuse an application, the Minister shall serve on the applicant a notice in writing—

(*a*) specifying the grounds on which the Minister proposes to refuse the application, and

(b) informing the applicant that the applicant may, within 21 days after the serving of the notice, make written representations to the Minister showing why the Minister should grant the application.

(3) Not later than 21 days after a notice is served on an applicant under *subsection (2)*, the applicant may make written representations to the Minister showing why the Minister should grant the application.

(4) The Minister may refuse an application only after having considered any representations made by the applicant in accordance with *subsection (3)*.

(5) As soon as practicable after refusing an application, the Minister shall serve a written notice of the refusal on the applicant. The notice shall include a statement—

(a) setting out the grounds on which the Minister has refused the application, and

(b) informing the applicant that—
   (i) the applicant may appeal to an Appeal Tribunal against the refusal, and
   (ii) if the applicant proposes to appeal to an Appeal Tribunal against the refusal, the applicant may, within one month after being served with the notice of refusal, serve a notice of intention to appeal on the Minister, in the form provided or specified by the Minister.

(6) If the Minister does not refuse the application, he or she shall grant it and, on granting the application, the Minister shall—

(a) record the appropriate particulars of the holder of the authorisation in the register of persons authorised to carry on business as a trust or company service provider, and

(b) issue the applicant with an authorisation that authorises the holder of the authorisation to carry on business as a trust or company service provider.

Minister may impose conditions when granting an application for an authorisation

90.—(1) In granting an application for an authorisation under this Chapter, the Minister may impose on the holder of the authorisation any conditions that the Minister considers necessary for the proper and orderly regulation of the holder's business as a trust or company service provider and, in particular, for preventing the business from being used to carry out money laundering or terrorist financing.

(2) The Minister shall specify any such conditions in the authorisation granted to the holder or in one or more documents annexed to that authorisation.

(3) If, under this section, the Minister imposes any conditions on an authorisation, the Minister shall serve on the holder of the authorisation,

together with the authorisation, a written notice of the imposition of the conditions that includes a statement—

(*a*) setting out the grounds on which the Minister has imposed the conditions, and
(*b*) informing the holder that—
    (i) the holder may appeal to an Appeal Tribunal against the imposition of any of the conditions, and
    (ii) if the holder proposes to appeal to an Appeal Tribunal against the imposition of any of the conditions, the holder may, within one month after being served with the notice of the imposition of conditions, serve a notice of intention to appeal on the Minister, in the form provided or specified by the Minister.

Terms of authorisation

91.—(1) An authorisation comes into force on the day on which the authorisation is granted, or, if a later date is specified in the authorisation, on that later date, whether or not an appeal against any conditions of the authorisation is made under *section 100*.

(2) An authorisation remains in force, unless sooner revoked under this Chapter, for a period of 3 years from the date on which it comes into force.

(3) A reference in this section to an authorisation does not include a reference to an authorisation that is renewed under *section 92*.

Renewal of authorisation

92.—(1) The Minister may renew an authorisation on the application of the holder of the authorisation unless the authorisation has been revoked under this Chapter.

(2) *Sections 88* to *90* apply, with any necessary modifications, in relation to an application for the renewal of an authorisation.

(3) An application for the renewal of an authorisation shall be made not less than 10 weeks before the end of the period for which it was granted.

(4) In addition to the grounds specified in *section 89* (as applied by *subsection (2)*), the Minister may refuse to grant a renewed authorisation on the grounds that the application for renewal has been made less than 10 weeks before the end of the period for which the authorisation was granted.

(5) If an application for the renewal of an authorisation is made within the time provided for in *subsection (3)* and is not determined by the Minister before the end of the period for which the authorisation was granted, the authorisation remains in force until the date on which the application is determined.

(6) A renewed authorisation comes into force on—

(*a*) in a case where *subsection (5)* applies, the date on which the application is determined, or (*b*) in any other case, the day immediately following the end of the period for which the authorisation that it renews was granted or last renewed, as the case may be.

(7) A renewed authorisation, unless sooner revoked under this Chapter, remains in force for a period of 3 years from the date on which it comes into force under *subsection (6)*.

(8) *Subsections (6)* and *(7)* have effect whether or not an appeal against any conditions of the authorisation is made under *section 100*.

Minister may amend authorisation

93.—(1) The Minister may amend an authorisation granted under this Chapter by varying, replacing or revoking any conditions or by adding a new condition if the Minister considers that the variation, replacement, revocation or addition is necessary for the proper and orderly regulation of the business of the holder of the authorisation as a trust or company service provider and, in particular, for preventing the business from being used to carry out money laundering or terrorist financing.

(2) If the Minister proposes to amend an authorisation under this section, the Minister shall serve on the holder of the authorisation a notice in writing informing the holder of the Minister's intention to amend the authorisation.

(3) The notice shall—

(*a*) specify the proposed amendment, and
(*b*) inform the holder that the holder may, within 21 days after service of the notice, make written representations to the Minister showing why the Minister should not make that amendment.

(4) Not later than 21 days after a notice is served under *subsection (2)* on the holder of an authorisation, the holder may make written representations to the Minister showing why the Minister should not amend the authorisation.

(5) The Minister may amend an authorisation only after having considered any representations to the Minister made in accordance with *subsection (4)* showing why the Minister should not amend the authorisation.

(6) The Minister shall serve written notice of any amendment of an authorisation on the holder of the authorisation. The notice shall include a statement—

(*a*) setting out the grounds on which the Minister has amended the authorisation, and
(*b*) informing the holder that—
    (i) the holder may appeal to an Appeal Tribunal against the amendment, and

(ii) if the holder proposes to appeal to an Appeal Tribunal against the amendment, the holder may, within one month after being served with the notice of amendment, serve a notice of intention to appeal on the Minister, in the form provided or specified by the Minister.

(7) The amendment of an authorisation under this section takes effect from the date of the notice of amendment or, if a later date is specified in the notice, from that date, whether or not an appeal against the amendment is made under *section 100*.

Offence to fail to comply with conditions or prescribed requirements
94.—(1) The holder of an authorisation commits an offence if the holder fails to comply with—

(*a*) any condition of the authorisation, or
(*b*) any prescribed requirements.

(2) A person who commits an offence under this section is liable—

(*a*) on summary conviction, to a fine not exceeding €2,000, or
(*b*) on conviction on indictment, to a fine not exceeding €100,000.

(3) The Minister may prescribe requirements for the purposes of *subsection (1)(b)* only if the Minister is satisfied that it is necessary to do so for the proper and orderly regulation of the business of trust or company service providers and, in particular, for preventing such businesses from being used to carry out money laundering or terrorist financing.

Holder of authorisation to ensure that principal officers and beneficial owners are fit and proper persons
95.—(1) The holder of an authorisation shall take reasonable steps to ensure that the following persons are fit and proper persons:

(*a*) in a case where the holder of the authorisation is a body corporate, a partnership or an individual carrying on business as a trust or company service provider as a partner in a partnership, any principal officer of the body corporate or partnership (as the case may be);
(*b*) any person who is a beneficial owner of the business concerned.

(2) A person who commits an offence under this section is liable—

(*a*) on summary conviction, to a fine not exceeding €2,000, or
(*b*) on conviction on indictment, to a fine not exceeding €100,000.

Section Note
Section 95(2) provides the penalties for committing an offence under section 95 but section 95 does not expressly establish an offence.

Revocation of authorisation by Minister on application of holder

96.—The Minister shall revoke an authorisation on the application of the holder of the authorisation, but only if satisfied that the holder of the authorisation has fully complied with each of the following:

(*a*) any conditions of the authorisation;

(*b*) any prescribed requirements referred to in *section 94*;

(*c*) *section 95*;

(*d*) *section 98*;

(*e*) *section 106*.

Revocation of authorisation other than on application of holder

97.—(1) The Minister may revoke an authorisation only if the Minister has reasonable grounds to be satisfied of any of the following:

(*a*) the holder of the authorisation has not commenced to carry on business as a trust or company service provider within 12 months after the date on which the authorisation was granted;

(*b*) the holder of the authorisation has not carried on such a business within the immediately preceding 6 months;

(*c*) the authorisation was obtained by means of a false or misleading representation;

(*d*) any of the following persons is not a fit and proper person:

   (i) the holder of the authorisation;

   (ii) in a case where the holder of the authorisation is a body corporate, a partnership or an individual carrying on business as a trust or company service provider as a partner in a partnership, any principal officer of the body corporate or partnership (as the case may be);

   (iii) any person who is a beneficial owner of the business concerned;

(*e*) the holder of the authorisation has contravened or is contravening the obligations imposed on trust or company service providers, as designated persons, under this Part;

(*f*) the holder of the authorisation has contravened or is contravening any of the following:

   (i) a condition of the authorisation;

   (ii) a prescribed requirement referred to in *section 94*;

   (iii) *section 95*;

   (iv) *section 98*;

   (v) *section 106*;

(*g*) the holder of the authorisation is so structured, or the business of the holder is so organised, that the holder is not capable of being regulated under this Chapter or as a designated person under this Part;

(*h*) in a case where the holder of the authorisation is a body corporate, the body corporate is being wound up;

(*i*) in a case where the holder of the authorisation is a partnership, the partnership is dissolved by the death or bankruptcy of a partner or because of the operation of a provision of the Partnership Act 1890 or otherwise;

(j) in a case where any person referred to in *paragraph (d)* has been authorised to carry on business as a trust or company service provider in another Member State, an authority of the other Member State that performs functions similar to those of the Minister under this Chapter has terminated the authority of the person to carry on business as a trust or company service provider in the other Member State;

(k) in a case where the holder of the authorisation is a subsidiary of a body corporate that is authorised to carry on business as a trust or company service provider in another Member State, an authority of the other Member State that performs functions similar to those of the Minister under this Chapter has terminated the authority of the body corporate to carry on business as a trust or company service provider in the other Member State.

(2) If the Minister proposes to revoke an authorisation under this section, the Minister shall serve on the holder of the authorisation a notice in writing informing the holder of the Minister's intention to revoke the authorisation.

(3) The notice shall—

(a) specify the grounds on which the Minister proposes to revoke the authorisation, and

(b) inform the holder that the holder may, within 21 days after service of the notice, make written representations to the Minister showing why the Minister should not revoke the authorisation.

(4) Not later than 21 days after a notice is served under *subsection (2)* on the holder of an authorisation, the holder may make written representations to the Minister showing why the Minister should not revoke the authorisation.

(5) The Minister may revoke the authorisation only after having considered any representations made by the holder of the authorisation in accordance with *subsection (4)*.

(6) As soon as practicable after revoking an authorisation under this section, the Minister shall serve written notice of the revocation on the person who was the holder of the authorisation. The notice shall include a statement—

(a) setting out the reasons for revoking the authorisation, and

(b) informing the holder that—

(i) the holder may appeal to an Appeal Tribunal against the revocation, and

(ii) if the holder proposes to appeal to an Appeal Tribunal against the revocation, the holder may, within one month after being served with the notice of revocation, serve a notice of intention to appeal on the Minister in the form provided or specified by the Minister.

(7) The revocation of an authorisation under this section takes effect from the date of the notice of revocation or, if a later date is specified in the notice, from that date, whether or not an appeal against the revocation is made under *section 100*.

Direction not to carry out business other than as directed

98.—(1) If the Minister reasonably believes that there may be grounds for revoking an authorisation under *section 97*, the Minister may serve on the holder of the authorisation a direction in writing prohibiting the holder from carrying on business as a trust or companyservice provider other than in accordance with conditions specified by the Minister.

(2) The Minister shall include in a direction under this section a statement—

(a) setting out the Minister's reasons for giving the direction,
(b) informing the holder of the authorisation concerned that—
   (i) the holder may appeal to an Appeal Tribunal against the direction, and
   (ii) if the holder proposes to appeal to an Appeal Tribunal against the direction, the holder may, within one month after being served with the direction, serve a notice of intention to appeal on the Minister in the form provided or specified by the Minister, and

(c) specifying the conditions with which the holder of the authorisation is required to comply.

(3) The Minister may, by notice in writing served on the holder of the authorisation concerned, amend or revoke a direction given under this section.

(4) Without prejudice to the generality of *subsection (3)*, the Minister may, by notice in writing given to the holder of the authorisation concerned, extend the period during which a direction remains in force by a further period or periods not exceeding 6 months.

(5) A direction under this section takes effect from the date on which it is given or, if a later date is specified in the direction, from that date, whether or not an appeal against the direction is made under *section 100*.

(6) A direction under this section ceases to have effect—

(a) at the end of the period, not exceeding 6 months, specified in the direction, or if the period is extended under *subsection (4)*, at the end of the extended period, or
(b) on the revocation of the holder's authorisation under this Chapter,

whichever occurs first.

(7) A person who contravenes a direction given under this section, or fails to comply with a condition contained in the direction, commits an offence.

(8) A person who commits an offence under this section is liable—

(*a*) on summary conviction, to a fine not exceeding €5,000, or

(*b*) on conviction on indictment, to a fine or imprisonment for a term not exceeding 5 years (or both).

Minister to publish notice of revocation or direction

99.—As soon as practicable after revoking an authorisation under *section 96* or *97*, or giving a direction under *section 98*, the Minister shall publish in *Iris Oifigiúil* a notice giving particulars of the revocation or direction.

Appeals against decisions of Minister

100.—(1) In this section, "appealable decision" means a decision of the Minister under—

(*a*) *section 89* to refuse an application for an authorisation,

(*b*) *section 89*, as applied by *section 92*, to refuse an application for the renewal of an authorisation,

(*c*) *section 90* to impose conditions on an authorisation,

(*d*) *section 90*, as applied by *section 92*, to impose conditions on an authorisation that is renewed,

(*e*) *section 93* to amend an authorisation,

(*f*) *section 97* to revoke an authorisation, or

(*g*) *section 98* to serve a direction on the holder of an authorisation.

(2) A person aggrieved by an appealable decision may, within one month after being served with notice of the decision, serve a notice of the person's intention to appeal against the decision on the Minister in the form provided or specified by the Minister.

(3) On receipt of the notification, the Minister shall refer the matter to an Appeal Tribunal established under *section 101*.

(4) The Appeal Tribunal may invite the person and the Minister to make written submissions to it in relation to the appeal.

(5) The Appeal Tribunal shall notify the person, in writing, of the following matters:

(*a*) the date and time of the hearing of the appeal;

(*b*) that the person may attend the hearing;

(*c*) that the person may be represented at the hearing by a barrister, solicitor or agent.

(6) An Appeal Tribunal may refuse to hear, or continue to hear, an appeal under this section if it is of the opinion that the appeal is vexatious, frivolous, an abuse of process or without substance or foundation.

(7) The Appeal Tribunal shall (unless the appeal is withdrawn, or discontinued or dismissed under *subsection (6)*) determine the appeal by—

(*a*) affirming the decision of the Minister to which the appeal relates, or

(*b*) substituting its determination for that decision.

(8) The Appeal Tribunal shall notify its determination in writing to the Minister and the person appealing.

(9) Within 3 months after the date on which an appeal is determined by an Appeal Tribunal, the Minister or person who appealed may appeal to the High Court on any question of law arising from the determination.

Appeal Tribunals

101.—(1) The Minister may, by order, establish, for a specified period, an Appeal Tribunal or more than one Appeal Tribunal to adjudicate on appeals under *section 100*.

(2) An Appeal Tribunal shall be independent in the performance of its functions.

(3) The Minister may appoint a person who is a practising barrister or solicitor of not less than 7 years' standing to be a member of and constitute an Appeal Tribunal.

(4) The appointment shall be subject to such terms and conditions, including remuneration, as the Minister may determine with the consent of the Minister for Finance.

(5) A person constituting an Appeal Tribunal may at any time resign by a letter sent to the Minister, and the resignation shall take effect on the date on which the Minister receives the letter.

(6) The Minister may, at any time, revoke an appointment of a person under this section for stated misbehaviour or if, in the opinion of the Minister, the person has become incapable through ill health or otherwise of effectively performing the functions of an Appeal Tribunal.

(7) An Appeal Tribunal may determine its own procedure, subject to *section 101* and to any general directions given to Appeal Tribunals by the Minister in the interests of securing consistency of procedures in relation to appeals under this Chapter.

Provision of information by Garda Síochána as to whether or not person is fit and proper person

102.—(1) The Minister may request the Commissioner of the Garda Síochána to provide any information that is required to assist the Minister in determining, for the purposes of this Chapter, whether or not any of the following persons is a fit and proper person:

(*a*) the holder or proposed holder of an authorisation;

(*b*) in a case where the holder or proposed holder of the authorisation is a body corporate, a partnership or an individual carrying on, or proposing to carry on, business as a trust or company service provider as a partner in a partnership, any principal officer of the body corporate or partnership (as the case may be);

(c) any person who is a beneficial owner of the business of the holder or proposed holder of the authorisation concerned.

(2) Notwithstanding any other enactment or rule of law, the Commissioner of the Garda Síochána shall provide the Minister with information in accordance with a request of the Minister under this section.

Extension of powers under *Chapter 8* for purposes related to this Chapter

103.—(1) The functions of a State competent authority, in relation to designated persons, under *Chapter 8*, may be performed by the Minister to assist him or her in carrying out functions in relation to trust or company service providers under this Chapter.

(2) For that purpose, *sections 66* to *83* apply with any necessary modifications, including the following:

(a) a relevant authorised officer has, in respect of trust or company service providers within the meaning of this Chapter, all of the functions that an authorised officer appointed by a State competent authority under *section 72* has in respect of designated persons;

(b) a judge of the District Court, in the case of an application under *section 78* by a relevant authorised officer in respect of a trust or company service provider, has all of the functions that such a judge has, in the case of a similar application under that section by an authorised officer appointed by a State competent authority under *section 72*, in respect of a designated person;

(c) *section 79* applies so as to enable a relevant authorised officer to be accompanied and assisted in the exercise of the officer's powers as referred to in that section;

(d) *section 80* applies to a person who engages in conduct, referred to in that section, in relation to—

    (i) a relevant authorised officer, and

    (ii) any person accompanying and assisting the officer in accordance with *section 79* as applied by *paragraph (c)*.

(3) This section has effect whether or not the Minister is the State competent authority for any class of trust or company service providers.

(4) In this section "relevant authorised officer" means an authorised officer appointed by the Minister under *section 72*, as applied by this section.

Register of persons holding auithorisations

104.—(1) The Minister shall establish and maintain a register of persons authorised under this Chapter to carry on business as a trust or company service provider containing—

(a) the name and the address of the principal place of business of each person authorised to carry on business as a trust or company service provider, and (*b*) such other information as may be prescribed.

(2) The register may be in book form, electronic form or such other form as the Minister may determine. The register may be maintained in an electronic, mechanical or other non-written form only if it is capable of being reproduced in a written form.

(3) The Minister shall maintain the register at an office of the Department.

(4) Members of the public are entitled, without charge, to inspect the register during the ordinary business hours of the Department.

(5) A member of the public is entitled to obtain a copy of the register or of an entry in a register on payment of such reasonable copying charges as may be prescribed (if any).

(6) The holder of an authorisation to whom an entry in the Register relates shall, as soon as practicable after the holder becomes aware of any error in the entry, or any change in circumstances that is likely to have a bearing on the accuracy of the entry, give notice in writing to the Minister of the error or change in circumstances, as the case may be.

(7) In any legal proceedings, a certificate purporting to be signed by the Minister and stating that a person—

(*a*) is recorded in the Register as the holder of an authorisation,

(*b*) is not recorded in the Register as the holder of an authorisation,

(*c*) was recorded in the Register as being, at a specified date or during a specified period, the holder of an authorisation, or

(*d*) was not recorded in the Register as being, at a specified date or during a specified period, the holder of an authorisation, is evidence of the matter referred to in *paragraph (a), (b), (c)* or *(d)* (as the case may be), and is taken to have been signed by the person purporting to have signed it, unless the contrary is shown.

(8) The Minister may prescribe particulars for the purposes of *subsection (1)(b)* or *section 105* only if satisfied that those particulars reasonably relate to the business of trust or company service providers or to the regulation of the business of trust or company service providers under this Part.

Section Note
At the time of writing, it is intended that the register referred to in s.104 will be available online on the Department of Justice website (the relevant page being under construction).

Minister to publish list of persons holding authorisations
105.—The Minister shall, not less frequently than once during every period of 12 months after the commencement of this section, publish in *Iris*

Oifigiúil a list of persons holding authorisations, together with other prescribed particulars (if any).

Holders of authorisations to retain certain records

106.—(1) The holder of an authorisation shall—

(a) retain at an office or other premises in the State such records as may be specified by the Minister, and

(b) notify the Minister in writing of the address of any office or other premises where those records are retained.

(2) The requirement imposed by *subsection (1)* is in addition to, and not in substitution for, any other requirements imposed under any other enactment or rule of law with respect to the retention of records by the holder of an authorisation, including the requirements specified in *section 55*.

(3) The holder of an authorisation shall retain the records referred to in *subsection (1)* for a period of not less than 6 years after—

(a) in the case of a record made in relation to a customer of the holder, the last dealing with the customer, or

(b) in any other case, the record is made.

(4) The holder of an authorisation may keep the records referred to in *subsection (1)* wholly or partly in an electronic, mechanical or other non-written form only if they are capable of being reproduced in a written form.

(5) The obligations that are imposed on a holder of an authorisation under this section continue to apply to a person who has been the holder of an authorisation, but has ceased to hold an authorisation or to carry on business as a trust or company service provider.

(6) A requirement for the holder of an authorisation that is a body corporate to retain any record under this section applies to any body corporate that is a successor to, or a continuation of, the body corporate.

(7) The Minister may make regulations prescribing requirements relating to the retention of records referred to in this section of a body corporate that is wound up or a partnership that is dissolved.

(8) A person who fails to comply with this section commits an offence and is liable—

(a) on summary conviction, to a fine not exceeding €5,000 or imprisonment for a term not exceeding 12 months (or both), or

(b) on conviction on indictment, to a fine or imprisonment for a term not exceeding 5 years (or both).

Section Note

The reference to a six-year retention period in s.106(3) sits well with s.56(1)(a) but somewhat uneasily with, for example, s.55(4). Off hand it seems undesirable to have varying retention periods prescribed in a single enactment and it may be that an upwards harmonisation to a standard six-year retention period throughout the Act would have been preferable. Failure by a person to comply with s.106 is a criminal offence. (On offences generally under the Act, see the table of offences arising under the Act (and the penalties for same) in Appendix 2 of this text).

CHAPTER 10

Other

General Note

Chapter 10 contains a trio of miscellaneous measures concerned respectively with: (1) the approval by the Minister for Justice and Law Reform of guidelines for the purpose of guiding designated persons on the application of Pt.4 of the Act to such persons; (2) the delegation by the Minister of any of his functions under Ch.8 or 9 or s.109 of the Act; and (3) the registration of persons who effectively direct private members' clubs.

Guidelines

107.—(1) The Minister may, after consulting with the Minister for Finance, approve guidelines for the purpose of guiding designated persons on the application of this Part to those designated persons.

(2) It is a defence to an offence under this Part for the defendant to prove that he or she took all reasonable steps and exercised all due diligence to avoid committing the offence.

(3) In determining whether a defendant took all such reasonable steps and exercised all such due diligence, a court may have regard to any guidelines applying in relation to the person that have been approved by the Minister under this section and are in force, but nothing in this section limits the matters that a court may have regard to in determining whether a defendant took all reasonable steps and exercised all due diligence to avoid committing an offence.

Section Note

Under s.107(1), the Minister for Justice and Law Reform may (after consulting with the Minister for Finance) approve guidelines for the purpose of guiding designated persons on the application of Pt.4 of the Act to such persons. The particular significance of guidelines approved under s.107 is that a court may, per s.107(3) of the Act, have regard to any such current approved guidelines (where applicable to a particular designated person) in determining whether such designated person (as defendant) took all reasonable steps and exercised all due diligence to avoid committing an offence under the Act, the taking of all such steps joined with the exercise of all due diligence being a defence to an offence under Pt.4 of the Act (per s.107(2)). A prudent designated person would therefore be well-advised generally to comply with any applicable guidelines approved under s.107. That said, compliance with such guidelines is not a requirement of the Act and a court in making the determination referred to in s.107(3) need not have regard (and need not have regard solely) to whether there has been compliance with any such guidelines. Indeed a person could conceivably be acquitted of an offence under Pt.4 even though such person was demonstrably not in compliance with applicable approved guidelines. It is possible that compliance with any such guidelines as are approved and applicable to a class of designated person will in effect become mandatory if the relevant competent authority gauges its reporting and compliance direction obligations under ss.63 and 71 by reference to same. At the time of writing, certain draft guidelines (or "Guidance Notes" as they are styled) pertaining to banking, credit unions, insurance, investment funds, stockbrokers, are the subject of a consultation exercise by the Central Bank. For a consideration of certain aspects of the draft guidelines pertaining to banking, see Barrett, M., "Customer Identification under Ireland's new Anti-Money Laundering and Terrorist Financing Legislation", Parts I and II at [2010] J.I.B.L.R. 502 and 568.

The guidelines were referred to in s.107 of the Bill as "codes of practice" but the Minister for Justice, Equality and Law Reform announced as early as the Second Stage Reading of the Bill before the Dáil, in effect the first consideration of the Bill by either House of the Oireachtas, that he intended to bring forward an amendment to describe the codes as guidelines "which is closer to the terminology in use" (695(2) *Díospóireachtaí Parlaiminte* (Dáil Éireann) (19.11.2009), p.261), the then current terminology being to refer to such guidelines as "guidance notes", the 'guidelines' applicable to credit institutions, for example, being the "Guidance Notes for Credit Institutions" published under the auspices of The Money Laundering Steering Committee in May 2003).

Minister may delegate certain functions under this Part

108.—(1) The Minister may, by instrument in writing, delegate any of the Minister's functions under *Chapter 8* or *9*, or under *section 109*, to a named officer or an officer of a particular class or description.

(2) A delegation under this section may be made subject to such conditions or limitations as to the performance of any of the functions delegated, or as to time or circumstance, as may be specified in the instrument of delegation.

(3) The Minister may, by instrument in writing, revoke a delegation under this section.

(4) A function delegated under this section may, while the delegation remains unrevoked, be performed by the delegate in accordance with the terms of the delegation.

(5) The Minister may continue to perform any functions delegated under this section.

(6) Nothing in this section shall be construed as affecting the application to this Act of the general law concerning the imputing of acts of an officer of a Minister of the Government to the Minister of the Government.

(7) In this section, "officer" means an officer of the Minister who is an established civil servant for the purposes of the Civil Service Regulation Act 1956.

Registration of persons directing private members' clubs

109.—(1) A person who is a designated person pursuant to *section 25(1)(h)* shall register with the Minister in accordance with such procedures as may be prescribed or otherwise imposed by the Minister.

(2) A person who is required to register under this section commits an offence if the person fails to do so and is liable—

(*a*) on summary conviction, to a fine not exceeding €5,000 or imprisonment for a term not exceeding 12 months (or both), or

(*b*) on conviction on indictment to a fine or imprisonment for a term not exceeding 5 years (or both).

(3) The following particulars shall be entered into a register established and maintained by the Minister for the purposes of this section:

(*a*) the name of each designated person who registers under this section;

(*b*) the name and address of the premises of the private members' club in relation to which the person is a designated person;

(*c*) any prescribed information as may be reasonably required by the Minister for the purposes of this Act.

(4) The register may be in book form, electronic form or such other form as the Minister may determine. The register may be maintained in an electronic, mechanical or other non-written form only if it is capable of being reproduced in a written form.

(5) The Minister shall maintain the register at an office of the Department.

(6) The Minister may prescribe particulars for the purposes of *subsection (3)(c)* only if satisfied that those particulars reasonably relate to the business or regulation of persons directing members' clubs as designated persons.

Section Note

The definition of "designated person" in s.25(1) includes, at sub-s.(h), "a person who effectively directs a private members' club at which gambling activities are carried on, but only in respect of those gambling activities". There has been a proliferation in Ireland in recent years of private members' clubs providing casino-style games to club members on the basis that the provisions of the Gaming and Lotteries Act 1956

(No.2 of 1956), as amended, do not apply to *bona fide* members' clubs. (see further the Report of the Casino Committee, "regulating Gaming in Ireland" (2008)). During the Second Stage reading of the Criminal Justice (Money Laundering and Terrorist Financing) Bill 2009, the Minister stated in this regard that:

> "A number of Deputies wanted to know why gaming clubs were involved....These private members' clubs are locations where large amounts of money could be put through, and it is only right and proper that they should be among the designated bodies, and regulated." (695(2) *Díospóireachtaí Parlaiminte* (Dáil Éireann) (19.11.2009), p.283).

Their inclusion within the definition of "designated person" for the purposes of the Act represents something of an enhancement of the anti-money laundering and anti-terrorist financing regime established by the Directive albeit that the Directive does make provision as regards casinos (which are "near relatives" of the Irish private members' club). Such an enhancement is permitted under Art.5 of the Directive.

Section 109 requires that such a designated person register with the Minister for Justice and Law Reform in accordance with such procedures as the Minister may prescribe or impose. Failure to so register is a criminal offence (per s.109(2)). (On offences generally under the Act, see the table of offences arising under the Act (and the penalties for same) in Appendix 2 of this text). The Minister is required to establish and maintain, at an office of the Department of Justice and Law Reform, a register of persons directing private members' clubs. At the time of writing it is intended that the register referred to in s.109 will be available online on the Department of Justice website. (The relevant page, at the time of writing, is under construction).

PART 5

Miscellaneous

General Note

Part 5 of the Act is made up mostly of the technical provisions and consequential amendments to legislation that are commonplace at the end of many enactments. Thus, s.110 makes provision for the service of notices and documents under the Act. Section 111 makes the often-found provision for the criminal liability of certain officers and other persons where an offence is committed by a body corporate or a person purporting to act on behalf of same or on behalf of an unincorporated body of persons. Section 112 is a "whistle-blowing" or "good faith reporting" provision. It provides that the good faith disclosure of certain information to a member of the Garda Síochána or to any person concerned in the investigation or prosecution of a money laundering or terrorist financing offence shall not be treated, for any purpose, as breaching any restriction on the disclosure of such information as may be imposed by any other enactment (*i.e.* other than the Act) or rule of law. Sections 113 to 122 make incidental and consequential amendments.

Service of documents

110.—(1) A notice or other document that is required or permitted, under this Act, to be served on or given to a person shall be addressed to the person by name and may be served or given to the person in one of the following ways:

(*a*) by delivering it to the person;

(*b*) by leaving it at the address at which the person ordinarily resides or carries on business;

(*c*) by sending it by post in a pre-paid registered letter to the address at which the person ordinarily resides or carries on business;

(*d*) if an address for service has been furnished, by leaving it at, or sending it by post in a pre-paid registered letter to, that address;

(*e*) in the case of a direction to an individual or body (whether incorporated or unincorporated) under *Part 3* not to carry out any specified service or transaction at a branch or place of business of the body or individual, by leaving it at, or by sending it by post in a pre-paid registered letter to, the address of the branch or place of business (as the case may be);

(*f*) if the person giving notice considers that notice should be given immediately and a fax machine is located at an address referred to in *paragraph (b), (c), (d)* or *(e)*, by sending it by fax to that machine, but only if the sender's fax machine generates a message confirming successful transmission of the total number of pages of the notice.

(2) For the purposes of this section—

(*a*) a company registered under the Companies Acts is taken to be ordinarily resident at its registered office, and

(*b*) any body corporate other than a company registered under the Companies Acts or any unincorporated body is taken to be ordinarily resident at its principal office or place of business in the State.

(3) Nothing in *subsection (1)(e)* prevents the serving or giving of a direction or other document for the purposes of *Part 3* under any other provision of this section.

(4) This section is without prejudice to any mode of service or of giving a notice or any other document provided for under any other enactment or rule of law.

(5) This section does not apply in relation to the service of a notice on the Minister referred to in *section 100(2)*.

Offences – directors and others of bodies corporate and unincorporated bodies

111.—Where an offence under this Act is committed by a body corporate or by a person purporting to act on behalf of a body corporate or on behalf of an unincorporated body of persons, and is proved to have been committed with the consent or connivance, or to be attributable to any wilful neglect, of a person who, when the offence is committed, is—

(*a*) a director, manager, secretary or other officer of the body, or a person purporting to act in that capacity, or

(*b*) a member of the committee of management or other controlling authority of the body, or a person purporting to act in that capacity, that person is taken to have also committed the offence and may be proceeded against and punished accordingly.

Disclosure of information in good faith

112.—(1) This section applies to the disclosure in good faith, to a member of the Garda Síochána or to any person who is concerned in the investigation or prosecution of an offence of money laundering or terrorist financing, of—

(*a*) a suspicion that any property has been obtained in connection with any such offence, or derives from property so obtained, or

(*b*) any matter on which such a suspicion is based.

(2) A disclosure to which this section applies shall not be treated, for any purpose, as a breach of any restriction on the disclosure of information imposed by any other enactment or rule of law.

Section Note

Section 112 is a "whistle-blowing" or "good faith reporting" provision. It provides that the disclosure in good faith of certain information to a member of the Garda Síochána or to any person concerned in the investigation or prosecution of a money laundering or terrorist financing offence shall not be treated, for any purpose, as breaching any restriction on the disclosure of such information as may be imposed by any other enactment (*i.e.* other than the Act) or rule of law. The exception is not limited to disclosures by designated persons but instead applies to all disclosures of the types mentioned. The disclosures to which the protection of s.112 extends are good faith disclosures of: (a) a suspicion that any property has been obtained in connection with any offence of money laundering or terrorist financing, or derives from property so obtained; and (b) any matter on which suspicion is based. The protection would not appear, for example, to extend to a disclosure of a suspicion arising in connection with any of the many offences under the Act that is not an offence of money laundering or terrorist financing proper. As mentioned in the context of s.47, s.112 was the subject of some debate (an extract from which follows) at the Report and Final Stage Reading of the Bill by the Dáil:

> "**Deputy Michael D'Arcy:** Is there a defence for somebody who has suspicion on reasonable grounds, acts honestly and with good intention in the belief that something is amiss, makes a report as a designated person but who is incorrect and the information turns out to be unfounded? Without some form of a defence people will be very cagey about reporting potential money laundering or funds being transferred for terrorist purposes.
>
> ...**Deputy Dermot Ahern:** To give a simple answer, section 112 on disclosure of information in good faith protects people. Each case will be determined on its merits by a court but section 112 applies to the disclosure in good faith, to a member of the Garda Síochána or to any person who is concerned in the investigation or prosecution of an offence and the section states that a disclosure to which the section applies shall not be treated as a breach of any restriction on the disclosure of information imposed by any other enactment. It would take care of the situation to which Deputy D'Arcy refers." (702(3) *Díospóireachtaí Parlaiminte* (Dáil Éireann) (17.2.2010), p.571).

At a later stage of the debate referred to above, the Minister was again questioned about the need for immunity from liability where disclosures are made. (See the question of Deputy Joanna Tuffy at 702(3) *Díospóireachtaí Parlaiminte* (Dáil Éireann) (17.2.2010), p.572). In reply, the Minister indicated that the Government's rationale in this regard was that civil or criminal liability could not arise unless there was a breach of an enactment or rule of law.

Section 112 has been considered, in the context of s.7(7) above with various other provisions of the Act that grant exceptions from liability in defined instances. If one compares it, however, with s.47 of the Act, the provision with which s.112 perhaps bears the greatest similarity, certain aspects of s.112 become more apparent. First, any person may seek to avail of the protection of s.112 provided the correct circumstances arise. Section 47 only applies to persons making a disclosure in accordance with Ch.4. Second, s.112 contains an express "good faith" requirement. Section 47 does not have this express good faith requirement but it does refer to a disclosure of information "in accordance with this Chapter" and it is difficult to see how a person not acting in good faith could, for example, know or (genuinely) suspect someone to be or have been engaged in an offence of money laundering or terrorist financing for the purposes of s.42, the provision that establishes the general reporting requirement in Ch.4. Third, s.112 applies at quite a late stage when an investigation or prosecution of an offence of money laundering or terrorist financing has commenced. By contrast, s.47 is concerned with exception from liability at the reporting stage, at which point no investigation or prosecution may have commenced. Fourth, the s.112 exception, when it arises, will apply to a disclosure to a particular member of the Garda Síochána or to any other of a defined class of persons which may or may not include the Revenue Commissioners or their staff. The s.47 exception, when it arises, will apply to a disclosure to either the Garda Síochána or the Revenue Commissioners done in accordance with Ch. 4 of Pt 4.

Amendment of Bail Act 1997

113.—The Schedule to the Bail Act 1997 is amended by inserting the following paragraph after paragraph 34 (inserted by section 48 of the Criminal Justice (Miscellaneous Provisions) Act 2009):

"*Money Laundering.*
35. Any offence under *Part 2* of the *Criminal Justice (Money Laundering and Terrorist Financing) Act 2010.*".

Section Note
The Schedule to the Bail Act 1997 lists certain offences which may constitute a "serious offence" for the purposes of that Act. Section 113 of the Act adds any offence under Pt.2 of the Act to the list.

Amendment of Central Bank Act 1942

114.—(1) In this section, "Act of 1942" means the Central Bank Act 1942.

(2) Section 33AK(5) (inserted by section 26 of the Central Bank and Financial Services Authority of Ireland Act 2003) of the Act of 1942 is amended by deleting paragraph (*n*).

(3) The Act of 1942 is amended by inserting the following after section 33AN (inserted by section 10 of the Central Bank and Financial Services Authority of Ireland Act 2004):

"Application of Part to credit unions.

33ANA.—(1) This Part applies in relation to—

(a) the commission or suspected commission by a credit union of a contravention of—

    (i) a provision of *Part 4* of the *Criminal Justice (Money Laundering and Terrorist Financing) Act 2010*,

    (ii) any direction given to the credit union under a provision of *Part 4* of that Act,

    (iii) any condition or requirement imposed on the credit union under a provision of *Part 4* of that Act or under any direction given to the credit union under a provision of that Part, or

    (iv) any obligation imposed on the credit union by this Part or imposed by the Regulatory Authority pursuant to a power exercised under this Part, and

(b) participation, by a person concerned in the management of a credit union, in the commission by the credit union of such a contravention.

(2) For those purposes—

(a) a reference in this Part to a regulated financial service provider includes a reference to a credit union,

(b) a reference in this Part to a prescribed contravention includes a reference to a contravention, by a credit union, of a provision, direction, condition, requirement or obligation referred to in subsection (1), and

(c) a reference in this Part to a person concerned in the management of a regulated financial service provider includes a reference to a person concerned in the management of a credit union.

(3) Nothing in this section limits the application of this Part in relation to matters other than those referred to in subsection (1).

(4) This section has effect notwithstanding anything to the contrary in section 184 of the Credit Union Act 1997.".

(4) Schedule 2 (substituted by section 31 of the Central Bank and Financial Services Authority of Ireland Act 2003) to the Act of 1942 is amended in Part 1 by inserting the following at the end of the Part:

"

No.–of 2010	Criminal Justice (Money Laundering and Terrorist Financing) Act 2010	Part 4

".

Section Note

Section 33AK(5) of the Central Bank Act 1942 empowers the Central Bank to disclose confidential information for the purpose of complying with certain reporting requirements of the Criminal Justice Act 1994.

Section 114(2) excises this now redundant provision. Section 114(3) of the Act adds a new s.33ANA to Central Bank Act 1942 which extends the enforcement provisions of Pt.III of that Act to contraventions of Pt.4 of the Act. Schedule 2 of the Central Bank Act 1942 lists certain measures under which the Irish Financial Services Regulatory Authority can perform the functions of the Central Bank and Financial Services Authority of Ireland. Section 114(4) adds to this list. Under the Central Bank Reform Act 2010 such responsibility is now given to the Central Bank.

Amendment of Courts (Supplemental Provisions) Act 1961

115.—Section 32A(1) of the Courts (Supplemental Provisions) Act 1961 (inserted by section 180 of the Criminal Justice Act 2006) is amended as follows:

(*a*) in paragraph (*d*) (inserted by section 18 of the Criminal Justice (Surveillance) Act 2009) by substituting "Criminal Justice (Surveillance) Act 2009;" for "Criminal Justice (Surveillance) Act 2009.";

(*b*) by inserting the following paragraph after paragraph (*d*):

"(*e*) any of the following powers under *Part 3* of the *Criminal Justice (Money Laundering and Terrorist Financing) Act 2010*:
  (i) the power to order a person not to carry out any service or transaction;
  (ii) the power to revoke an order referred to in subparagraph (i);
  (iii) the power to make an order in relation to property if considered essential to do so for the purpose of enabling—
    (I) the person who applies for the order to discharge the reasonable living and other necessary expenses incurred or to be incurred in respect of the person or the person's dependants, or
    (II) the person who applies for the order to carry on a business, trade, profession or other occupation to which any of the property relates.".

Section Note

Section 32A(1) of the Courts (Supplemental Provisions) Act 1961 is concerned with the exercise of certain powers by a District Court judge outside the relevant district court district. Section 115 of the Act, insofar as it refers to the Act, extends the application of s.32A to those powers under Pt.3 of the Act to which the text in s.115 refers.

Consequential amendment of Central Bank Act 1997

116.—Section 28 (substituted by section 27 of the Central Bank and Financial Services Authority of Ireland Act 2004) of the Central Bank Act 1997 is amended, in the definitions of "bureau de change business" and "money transmission service", by substituting the following for paragraphs (*a*) and (*b*) of those definitions:

"(*a*) by a person or body that is required to be licensed, registered or otherwise authorised by the Bank under a designated enactment (other than under this Part) or designated statutory instrument, or".

Section Note
Section 28 of the Central Bank Act 1997 defines certain terms employed in a Part of that enactment concerned with the supervision of regulated businesses. The effect of s.116 of the Act is to vary certain of those definitions.

Consequential amendment of Criminal Justice Act 1994

117.—(1) In this section, "Act of 1994" means the Criminal Justice Act 1994.

(2) Section 3(1) of the Act of 1994 is amended in the definition of "drug trafficking" by substituting the following for paragraph (*d*):

"(*d*) engaging in any conduct (whether or not in the State) in relation to property obtained, whether directly or indirectly, from anything done in relation to a controlled drug, being conduct that—
   (i) is an offence under *Part 2* of the *Criminal Justice (Money Laundering and Terrorist Financing) Act 2010* ("*Part 2* of the *Act of 2010*") or would have been an offence under that Part if the Part had been in operation at the time when the conduct was engaged in, or
   (ii) in the case of conduct in a place outside of the State, other than conduct referred to in subparagraph (i)—
      (I) would be an offence under *Part 2* of the *Act of 2010* if done in corresponding circumstances in the State, or
      (II) would have been an offence under that Part if done in corresponding circumstances in the State and if the Part had been in operation at the time when the conduct was engaged in, or".

(3) Section 3(1) of the Act of 1994 is amended in the definition of "drug trafficking offence" by substituting the following for paragraph (*e*):

"(*e*) an offence under *Part 2* of the *Criminal Justice (Money Laundering and Terrorist Financing) Act 2010*, or under section 31 of this Act (as in force before the commencement of that Part), in relation to the proceeds of drug trafficking,".

Section Note
Section 3(1) of the Criminal Justice Act 1994 defined various terms used in that Act. The effect of s.117(2) and (3) is to vary the definitions of "drug trafficking" and "drug trafficking offence" for the purposes of that Act.

Consequential amendment of Criminal Justice (Mutual Assistance) Act 2008

118.—Section 94(3) of the Criminal Justice (Mutual Assistance) Act 2008 is amended by substituting "*Part 2* of the *Criminal Justice (Money Laundering and Terrorist Financing) Act 2010*" for "section 31 of the Criminal Justice Act 1994, as substituted by section 21 of the Criminal Justice (Theft and Fraud Offences) Act 2001".

Section Note

The Criminal Justice (Mutual Assistance) Act 2008 is principally concerned with mutual assistance between Ireland and other States in criminal matters. Its enactment accords with various elements of the thirty-sixth to fortieth of the FATF 40 Recommendations which recommend, *inter alia*, that "Countries should rapidly, constructively and effectively provide the widest possible range of mutual legal assistance in relation to money laundering and terrorist financing investigations, prosecutions, and related proceedings" and that "Countries should ensure that their competent authorities provide the widest possible range of international cooperation to their foreign counterparts". (FATF, *FATF 40 Recommendations*, pp. 12ff). S.94(3) of the 2008 Act is concerned with the Treaty between the Government of Ireland and the Government of the United States of America on Mutual Assistance in Criminal Matters done at Washington, DC on 18 January 2001, as applied by the Instrument contemplated by Art.3(2) of the EU-US Agreement (*i.e.* the Agreement on Mutual Legal Assistance between the European Union and the United States of America, done at Washington DC, on 25 June 2003) as to the application of the US-Ireland (*sic*) Treaty and done at Dublin on 14 July 2005. S.118 inserts a reference to the Act in place of an existing reference to the Criminal Justice Act 1994.

Consequential amendment of Criminal Justice (Theft and Fraud Offences) Act 2001

119.—Section 40(1) of the Criminal Justice (Theft and Fraud Offences) Act 2001 is amended by substituting the following for the definition of "money laundering":

" 'money laundering' means an offence under *Part 2* of the *Criminal Justice (Money Laundering and Terrorist Financing) Act 2010*;".

Section Note

The Criminal Justice (Theft and Fraud Offences) Act 2001 was enacted in part to give effect to the Convention on the Protection of the European Communities' Financial Interests done at Brussels on 26 July 1995. As its title suggests this convention seeks to tackle fraud affecting the financial interests of the European Communities. Under the Convention, fraud affecting expenditure/revenue must be punishable by effective, proportionate and dissuasive criminal penalties in every EU Member State. The effect of s.119 is to amend the definition of "money laundering" in Pt.6 of that Act so as to refer to the Act.

Consequential amendment of Investor Compensation Act 1998

120.—(1) In this section, "Act of 1998" means the Investor Compensation Act 1998.

(2) Section 30(1) of the Act of 1998 is amended in the definition of "net loss" by substituting the following for subparagraph (iii):

"(iii) money or investment instruments arising out of transactions in respect of which an offence has been committed under the *Criminal Justice (Money Laundering and Terrorist Financing) Act 2010* ("Act of 2010"),

(iv) money or investment instruments arising out of transactions in respect of which an offence has been committed under a provision of Part IV of the Criminal Justice Act 1994 prior to the repeal of that provision by the *Act of 2010*,

(v) money or investment instruments arising out of transactions in respect of which an offence has been committed under a provision of section 57 or 58 of the Criminal Justice Act 1994 prior to the repeal of that provision by the *Act of 2010*, or

(vi) money or investment instruments arising out of transactions in respect of which there has been a criminal conviction, at any time, for money laundering, within the meaning of Directive 2005/60/EC of the European Parliament and of the Council of 26 October 2005 on the prevention of the use of the financial system for the purpose of money laundering and terrorist financing.[12]".

(3) Section 35 of the Act of 1998 is amended by substituting the following for subsection (3):

"(3) Notwithstanding the time limits provided for in subsections (1) and (2), the competent authority may direct the Company or a compensation scheme approved under section 25, as appropriate, to suspend any payment to an eligible investor, where the investor has been charged with any of the following offences, pending the judgment of a court in respect of the charge:

(a) an offence under the *Criminal Justice (Money Laundering and Terrorist Financing) Act 2010* ("Act of 2010");

(b) an offence committed, prior to the repeal by the *Act of 2010* of any of the following provisions of the Criminal Justice Act 1994, under that provision:

(i) a provision of Part IV;
(ii) section 57;
(iii) section 58;

(c) an offence otherwise arising out of, or relating to, money laundering, within the meaning of Directive 2005/60/EC of the European Parliament and of the Council of 26 October 2005 on the prevention of the use of the financial system for the purpose of money laundering and terrorist financing.[13]".

Section Note

Section 30(1) of the Investor Compensation Act 1998 excludes certain monies from the calculation of client loss (when calculating investor compensation). Section 120 revises that provision so that the legislation it refers to now includes the Act and the Directive. Section 35 of the

---

[12] OJ L309, 25.11.2005, p.15.
[13] OJ L309, 25.11.2005, p.15.

Investor Compensation Act 1998 is concerned with staying payment of investor compensation where an investor eligible to receive compensation is charged with certain offences under the Criminal Justice Act 1994. Section 120(3) makes further provision in this regard, extending s.35 so that it now also includes certain offences under the Act and of or relating to money laundering within the meaning of the Directive.

Consequential amendment of Taxes Consolidation Act 1997

121.—(1) In this section, "Act of 1997" means the Taxes Consolidation Act 1997.

(2) Section 898F (substituted by section 90 of, and Schedule 4 to, the Finance Act 2004) of the Act of 1997 is amended as follows:

(a) in subsection (3) by substituting "which is acceptable for the purposes of *Chapter 3* of *Part 4* of the *Criminal Justice (Money Laundering and Terrorist Financing) Act 2010*" for "it acquires by virtue of section 32 of the Criminal Justice Act 1994";

(b) in subsection (4) by substituting "which is acceptable for the purposes of *Chapter 3* of *Part 4* of the *Criminal Justice (Money Laundering and Terrorist Financing) Act 2010*" for "it acquires by virtue of section 32 of the Criminal Justice Act 1994";

(c) in subsection (5)(a) (substituted by section 124(1)(a) of the Finance Act 2006) by inserting "(or has done so, before the relevant commencement date, in accordance with this section as in force before that date)" after "in accordance with this section";

(d) by inserting the following paragraph after subsection (6)(a):

"(aa) A paying agent who—

   (i) before the relevant commencement date, established the identity and residence of an individual under this section as in force before that date, and

   (ii) was required, immediately before the relevant commencement date and as a result of paragraph (a), to continue to treat that individual as so identified and so resident, shall continue to treat that individual as so identified and so resident until such time as the paying agent is in possession, or aware, of information which can reasonably be taken to indicate that the individual has been incorrectly identified or is not so resident or has changed his or her residence.";

(e) in subsection (6)(b) by inserting "or (aa)" after "paragraph (a)";

(f) in subsection (7) by inserting "(or as established, before the relevant commencement date, in accordance with this section as in force before that date)" after "this section";

(g) by inserting the following subsection after subsection (7):

"(8) In this section, 'relevant commencement date' means the date on which *section 121(2)* of the *Criminal Justice (Money Laundering and Terrorist Financing) Act 2010* comes into operation.".

(3) Section 898G (substituted by section 90 of, and Schedule 4 to, the Finance Act 2004) of the Act of 1997 is amended as follows:

(a) in subsection (2) by substituting "*Chapter 3* of *Part 4* of the *Criminal Justice (Money Laundering and Terrorist Financing) Act 2010*" for "section 32 of the Criminal Justice Act 1994";

(b) in subsection (4)(b) by substituting "*Chapter 3* of *Part 4* of the *Criminal Justice (Money Laundering and Terrorist Financing) Act 2010*" for "section 32 of the Criminal Justice Act 1994";

(c) in subsection (5)(b)(iii) by substituting "*Chapter 3* of *Part 4* of the *Criminal Justice (Money Laundering and Terrorist Financing) Act 2010*" for "section 32 of the Criminal Justice Act 1994";

(d) in subsection (6)(a) (substituted by section 124(1)(b) of the Finance Act 2006) by inserting "(or has done so, before the relevant commencement date, in accordance with this section as in force before that date)" after "in accordance with this section";

(e) by inserting the following paragraph after subsection (8)(a):

"(aa) A paying agent who—
    (i) before the relevant commencement date, established the identity and residence of an individual under this section as in force before that date, and
    (ii) was required, immediately before the relevant commencement date and as a result of paragraph (a), to continue to treat that individual as so identified and so resident, shall continue to treat that individual as so identified and so resident until such time as the paying agent is in possession, or aware, of information which can reasonably be taken to indicate that the individual has been incorrectly identified or is not so resident or has changed his or her residence.";

(f) in subsection (8)(b) by inserting "or (aa)" after "paragraph (a)";

(g) in subsection (9) by inserting "(or as established, before the relevant commencement date, in accordance with this section as in force before that date)" after "this section";

(h) by inserting the following subsection after subsection (9): "(10) In this section, 'relevant commencement date' means the date on which *section 121(3)* of the *Criminal Justice (Money Laundering and Terrorist Financing) Act 2010* comes into operation.".

Section Note

Section 898F of the Taxes Consolidation Act 1997 sits in a Chapter of that Act concerned with the implementation of Council Directive 2003/48/EC of 3 June 2003 on Taxation of Savings Income in the Form of Interest Payments (O.J. L157, 26.6.2003, p.38) (the "Savings Tax Directive") and related matters. S.898F makes provision as regards establishing the identity and residence of certain individuals and applies the CDD standards of the Criminal Justice Act 1994 in this regard. Section 121(2) updates this legislation so as now to refer to the Act in this regard and makes certain related provision. Section 898G of the Taxes Consolidation Act makes provision as regards the identification obligation of paying agents in the context of certain contractual relations entered into and s.121(3) likewise updates the legislation in this regard so as to refer to the Act and make certain related provision.

Consequential amendment of Taxi Regulation Act 2003

122.—Section 36(1)(*f*) of the Taxi Regulation Act 2003 is amended by substituting "*Part 2* of the *Criminal Justice (Money Laundering and Terrorist Financing) Act 2010*" for "Part IV of the Criminal Justice Act 1994".

Section Note

Section 36(1)(f) of the Taxi Regulation Act 2003 provides for the mandatory disqualification of a "small public service vehicle" licence-holder where that licence-holder is convicted of one or more listed offences. Section 122 of the Act revises the 2003 Act so as to refer to an offence under Pt.2 of the Act.

SCHEDULE 1

Revocations of Statutory Instruments

Section 4

General Note

Section 4(2) of the Act revokes the statutory instruments specified in column (1) of Schedule 1 to the extent specified in column (3) of same. (Column (3) specifies that all of the relevant statutory instruments be revoked in their entirety). The regulations mentioned in Schedule 1 comprise the secondary legislation that staked out the anti-money laundering regime established under the Criminal Justice Act 1994:

- the Criminal Justice Act 1994 (Section 32(10)(a)) Regulations 1995 (S.I. No. 104 of 1995) (prescribed certain bodies as designated bodies for the purposes of s.32 of the Criminal Justice Act 1994);
- the Criminal Justice Act 1994 (Section 32(10)(b)) Regulations 1995 (S.I. No. 105 of 1995) (prescribed the acceptance of deposits and other repayable funds from the public as an activity to which s.32(2) of the Criminal Justice Act 1994 applied);
- the Criminal Justice Act 1994 (Section 32(10)(d)) Regulations 1995 (S.I. No. 106 of 1995) (prescribed various places for the purposes of s.32(6) of the Criminal Justice Act 1994);
- the Criminal Justice Act 1994 (Section 32(10)(b)) (No. 2) Regulations 1995 (S.I. No. 324 of 1995) (prescribed the purchase or sale of units of certain collective investment schemes as activities to which s.32(2) of the Criminal Justice Act 1994 applied);
- the Criminal Justice Act 1994 (Section 32(10)(a)) Regulations 2003 (S.I. No. 216 of 2003) (designated electronic money institutions within the meaning of the European Communities (Electronic Money) Regulations 2002 (S.I. No. 221 of 2002) as designated bodies under s.32(1) of the Criminal Justice Act 1994);
- the Criminal Justice Act 1994 (Section 32) Regulations 2003 (S.I. No. 242 of 2003) (prescribed certain bodies as designated bodies for the purposes of s.32 of the 1994 Act);
- the Criminal Justice Act 1994 (Section 32) (Amendment) Regulations 2003 (S.I. No. 416 of 2003) (amended the Criminal Justice Act 1994 (Section 32) Regulations (S.I. No. 242 of 2003) by substituting an amended version of Regulation 4 for the version contained in S.I. No. 242 of 2003);
- the Criminal Justice Act 1994 (Section 32) (Prescribed States or Countries) Regulations 2003 (S.I. No. 618 of 2003) (designated Argentina, Brazil, Mexico, Russia and South Africa for the purposes of s.32 of the Criminal Justice Act 1994);

- the Criminal Justice Act 1994 (Section 32) (Prescribed Activities) Regulations 2004 (S.I. No. 3 of 2004) (prescribed certain activities of certain designated bodies as activities that when carried out gave rise to identification obligations under s.32 of the Criminal Justice Act 1994); and
- the Criminal Justice Act 1994 (Section 32) (Prescribed States or Countries) Regulations 2004 (S.I. No. 569 of 2004) (designated Liechtenstein as a state for the purposes of s.32 of the Criminal Justice Act 1994).

Title of Instrument (1)	Number and Year (2)	Extent of Revocation (3)
Criminal Justice Act 1994 (Section 32(10)(a)) Regulations 1995	S.I. No. 104 of 1995	The whole Regulations.
Criminal Justice Act 1994 (Section 32(10)(b)) Regulations 1995	S.I. No. 105 of 1995	The whole Regulations.
Criminal Justice Act 1994 (Section 32(10)(d)) Regulations 1995	S.I. No. 106 of 1995	The whole Regulations.
Criminal Justice Act 1994 (Section 32(10)(b)) (No.2) Regulations 1995	S.I. No. 324 of 1995	The whole Regulations.
Criminal Justice Act 1994 (Section 32(10)(a)) Regulations 2003	S.I. No. 216 of 2003	The whole Regulations.
Criminal Justice Act 1994 (Section 32) Regulations 2003	S.I. No. 242 of 2003	The whole Regulations.
Criminal Justice Act 1994 (Section 32) (Amendment) Regulations 2003	S.I. No. 416 of 2003	The whole Regulations.
Criminal Justice Act 1994 (Section 32) (Prescribed States or Countries) Regulations 2003	S.I. No. 618 of 2003	The whole Regulations.
Criminal Justice Act 1994 (Section 32) (Prescribed Activities) Regulations 2004	S.I. No. 3 of 2004	The whole Regulations.
Criminal Justice Act 1994 (Section 32) (Prescribed States or Countries) Regulations 2004	S.I. No. 569 of 2004	The whole Regulations.

SCHEDULE 2

Annex I to Recast Banking Consolidation Directive
List of Activities Subject to Mutual Recognition

Section 24

General Note
Section 24 of the Act refers in the definition of "financial institution" to Annex I to the Recast Banking Consolidation Directive (as defined in s.24). The text of Annex I is set out in Schedule 2 of the Act.

(1) Acceptance of deposits and other repayable funds.

(2) Lending including, inter alia: consumer credit, mortgage credit, factoring, with or without recourse, financing of commercial transactions (including forfeiting).

(3) Financial leasing.

(4) Payment services as defined in Article 4(3) of Directive 2007/64/EC of the European Parliament and of the Council of 13 November 2007 on payment services in the internal market.[14]

(5) Issuing and administering other means of payment (e.g. travellers' cheques and bankers' drafts) insofar as this activity is not covered by point 4.

(6) Guarantees and commitments.

(7) Trading for own account or for account of customers in:
   (*a*) money market instruments (cheques, bills, certificates of deposit, etc.);
   (*b*) foreign exchange;
   (*c*) financial futures and options;
   (*d*) exchange and interest — rate instruments; or
   (*e*) transferable securities.

(8) Participation in securities issues and the provision of services related to such issues.

(9) Advice to undertakings on capital structure, industrial strategy and related questions and advice as well as services relating to mergers and the purchase of undertakings.

(10) Money broking.

(11) Portfolio management and advice.

(12) Safekeeping and administration of securities.

(13) Credit reference services.

(14) Safe custody services.

(15) Issuing electronic money.

---

[14] OJ L319, 15.12.2007, p.1.

The services and activities provided for in Sections A and B of Annex I to Directive 2004/39/EC of the European Parliament and of the Council of 21 April 2004 on markets in financial instruments, when referring to the financial instruments provided for in Section C of Annex I of that Directive, are subject to mutual recognition according to this Directive.

APPENDIX 1

Defined terms in the Act, the Directive and the Implementing Directive

Term defined	Act	Directive	Implementing Directive
"acceptable institution"	s.33(10)		
"Appeal Tribunal"	s.84		
"appealable decision"	s.100(1).		
"arrangement"	s.30(4).		
"authorisation"	s.84		
"barrister"	s.24(1)		
"beneficial owner"	s.24(1), ss. 26-30	Art.3(6)	
"business relationship"	s.24(1)	Art.3(9)	
"close associate"	s.37(10)		
"competent authority"	s.24(1), s.60		
"control"	s.28(4) and (5).		
"credit institution"	s.24(1)	Art.3(1)	
"criminal activity"		Art 3(4)	
"criminal conduct"	s.6		
"customer"	s.24(1)		
"Department"	s.24(1)		
"designated accountancy body"	s.24(1)		
"designated person"	ss.24(1), 25, 41, 49(4)		
"EEA State"	s.24(1)		
"Electronic Money Directive"	s.24(1)		
"entity"	s.30(4).		
"external accountant"	s.24(1)		
"financial institution"	s.24(1)	Art.3(2)	
"fit and proper person"	s.85		
"group"	s.24(1)		

APPENDIX 1 (*Continued*)

Term defined	Act	Directive	Implementing Directive
"immediate family member"	s.37(10).		Art.2(2).
"Implementing Directive"	s.2(1)		
"Insurance Mediation Directive"	s.24(1)		
"legal adviser"	s.48		
"Life Assurance Consolidation Directive"	s.24(1)		
"Markets in Financial Instruments Directive"	s.24(1)		
"member"	s.24(1)		
"Minister"	s.2(1)		
"money laundering"	s.2(1)	Art.1(2)	
"natural persons who are or have been entrusted with prominent public functions"			Art.2(1)
"occasional transaction"	s.24(1)		
"officer"	s.108(7)		
"payment service"	s.24(1)		
"Payment Services Directive"	s.24(1)		
"persons known to be close associates"			Art.2(3)
"politically exposed person" or "politically exposed persons"	s.37(10)	Art.3(8)	
"prescribed"	s.2(1)		
"principal officer"	s.84		
"proceeds of criminal conduct"	s.6		
"professional service provider"	s.24(1)		
"property"	s.2(1)	Art.3(3)	
"property service provider"	s.24(1)		
"public body"	s.24(1)		
"Recast Banking Consolidation Directive"	s.24(1)		
"regulated market"	s.24(1)		
"relevant authorised officer"	s.103(4).		
"relevant document"	s.86		

APPENDIX 1 (*Continued*)

Term defined	Act	Directive	Implementing Directive
"relevant independent legal professional"	s.24(1)		
"relevant information"	s.66(1)		
"relevant professional adviser"	s.24(1)		
"relevant third party"	s.40(1)		
"serious crimes"		Art.3(5)	
"shell bank"	s.59(6)	Art.3(10)	
"solicitor"	s.24(1)		
"specified customer"	s.34(4), (5); s.36(3)		
"specified official"	s.37(10)		
"specified product"	s.34(7), s.36(3)		
"State competent authority"	s.24(1), s.62		
"tax adviser"	s.24(1)		
"terrorist financing"	s.2(1)	Art.1(4)	
"Third Money Laundering Directive"	s.2(1)		
"third parties"		Art.16	
"transaction"	s.24(1)		
"trust"	s.28(1)		
"trust or company service provider"; or "trust and company service providers"	s.24(1), s.84	Art.3(7)	

APPENDIX 2

Offences under the Act and penalties for same

Provision of Act	Nature of offence	Penalty on summary conviction	Penalty on conviction on indictment
S.7	Money laundering in Ireland	A fine not exceeding €5,000 or imprisonment for a term not exceeding 12 months (or both)	A fine (no limit) or imprisonment for a term not exceeding 14 years (or both)
S.8	Money laundering outside Ireland in certain circumstances		
S.9	Attempts, outside Ireland, to commit s.7(1) offence in Ireland		
S.10	Aiding, abetting, counselling or procuring outside Ireland the commission of a s.7 offence in Ireland		
S.17	Direction or order not to carry out service or transaction		A fine (no limit) or imprisonment for a term not exceeding 5 years (or both)
S.33	Identification and verification of customers and beneficial owners		
S.35	Special measures applying to business relationships		
S.37	Enhanced CDD – politically exposed persons		
S.38	Enhanced CDD – correspondent banking relationships		
S.42	Requirement to report suspicious transactions		
S.43	Requirement to report transactions associated with certain places		
S.49	Tipping off		
S.54	Internal policies and procedures and training		
S.55	Keeping of records by designated persons		

APPENDIX 2 (*Continued*)

Provision of Act	Nature of offence	Penalty on summary conviction	Penalty on conviction on indictment
S.56	Measures for retrieval of information re. business relationships		
S.57	Branches and subsidiaries in non-EU Member States		
S.58	Anonymous accounts		
S.59	Shell banks		
S.67	Direction to furnish information/documents		
S.68	Direction to provide explanation of documents		
S.80	Offence to obstruct, interfere or fail to comply with request		
S.87	Unauthorised trust or company service provider		A fine (no limit) or imprisonment for a term not exceeding 5 years (or both)
S.94	Failure to comply with conditions or prescribed requirements	A fine not exceeding €2,000	A fine not exceeding €100,000
S.95	Ensure that principal officers and beneficial owners are fit and proper persons. (Section 95(2) provides the penalties for committing an offence under section 95 but section 95(1) does not expressly establish an offence.).		
S.98	Direction not to carry out business other than as directed	A fine not exceeding €5,000	A fine (no limit) or imprisonment for a term not exceeding 5 years (or both)
S.106	Holders of authorisations to retain certain records	A fine not exceeding €5,000 or imprisonment for a term not exceeding 12 months (or both)	
S.109	Registration of persons directing private members' clubs		

Index